D0512875

# VALSE DES FLEURS

*A day in St. Petersburg in 1868*

Sacheverell Sitwell

# VALSE DES FLEURS
*A day in St. Petersburg in 1868*

SICKLE MOON BOOKS
London
2000

Dedicated to
CYRIL W. BEAUMONT,
Critic of the Dance

First published by Faber & Faber in July 1941
Reprinted by Sickle Moon Books, 3 Inglebert Street,
Clerkenwell, London in 2000

© Estate of Sacheverell Sitwell

Foreword © Reresby Sitwell

Cover designed by Mick Keates using a watercolor on paper
of Princess Baryatinskaya's Ball by Grigori Grigorevich Gagarin
(1810-93) from the collection of the State Russian Museum,
St. Petersburg, Russia/Bridgeman Art Library.
The map printed on the half title page is taken from
T. Michell's 1868 Edition of Murray's Handbook for Travellers
in Russia, Poland and Finland.

This book printed and made for the publishers by GraphyCems.

ISBN 1-900209-10 (1)

# Foreword

*Valse des Fleurs* is the most readable and enjoyable of all the 135 books by Sacheverell Sitwell, in the opinion of his elder son. Written in the dreariest moments of the Second World War, it is a nostalgic and escapist essay, conjuring up the lost world of the "unlimited Autocrat of all the Russias", the Romanov Emperor, and the luxury of his court.

My father, affectionately known as "Sachie", invites us to a ball in the Winter Palace tonight. We are to see St. Petersburg in its snow and gilt: it is early one morning in 1868 and the giant Alexander II is Tsar. The *skorokhod*, the court runner, brings round the invitations by carriage. This allows for a description of great palaces here and near: green, pink and yellow, hundreds of yards long, standing stark against the pale green northern sky and the endless snowflakes. Many were constructed by foreign architects such as the Italian Rastrelli and Quarenghi or the Scottish Cameron.

Later in the morning a military parade takes place: the Tsar rides out from the central arch of the palace to review 40,000 men of his Imperial Guard. Salvoes of guns fire out from the fortress of St. Peter and St. Paul across the River Neva and, as each contingent marches past, its regimental band rings out frenzied renderings of the Tsarist national anthem *Boje Tsar Khrani*, composed for Nicholas I by Prince Lwow.

My father goes on to describe the splendid uniforms of the two rival regiments, of the Chevalier Gardes and the Gardes à Cheval, the accoutrements of Cuirasssiers and Lancers, the Horse Artillery, the Horse Grenadiers (a military oddity) and the be-whiskered Hussars in Hungarian guise. Countless regiments of infantry, from every corner of the ramshackle Empire, march past. These include the Preobrajenski Guards with their special privilege of entry into the Winter Palace. Strangest of all is the Pavlovski regiment of snub-nosed men founded by the mad Emperor Paul I, and confined to those who share his *kalmuck* features.

When this little book first appeared in the summer of 1941 it proved an unexpected success in the press: one misguided journalist hailed it all as wonderful propaganda for our Russian (Soviet) allies – not exactly the author's intention.

My father does not hesitate throughout this work to mention the sad plight of Polish patriots, who having survived the summary executions that followed their abortive uprising in 1863, had to suffer the rest of their lives in exile among the frozen wastes of Siberia. He also dwells on the barbarous conditions of the urban poor, the underclass of starving native Russians, former serfs and their offspring living in the freezing cellars beneath this most wondrous of all capitals.

The military review "ends with a furious charge of Cossacks" and we are taken by sledge around the sights of St. Petersburg, past the golden spire of the Admiralty and the colonnade of the Kazan cathedral. Another sledge draws up and a lady dressed in sables walks into a shop. In other sledges "there are women in crinolines, wrapped in Russian furs, sables, bearskins and the then rare silver fox and who, tonight, will be wearing jewels that no other Court can show". We can hardly wait for the Ball but we continue exploring the city to distant sounds of a gypsy band.

My father gives us a dissertation on Russian music and then harps back to the coronation of the Tsars in Moscow. Curious to relate, my grandfather, Sir George Sitwell, once visited Russia as a very young man, to attend the coronation of Nicholas II in 1895. I remember so well sitting on his knee, begging him to tell me, over and over again, this experience of a lifetime. In contrast, Sachie never set foot in Russia. His deep knowledge of the country, or at least of its erstwhile capital came from travel books, histories and memoirs. I have been there with Penelope as a tourist thirty years ago and then three times as a "guest lecturer" to groups of art-lovers visiting the city which was then still named Leningrad. But I must not keep you – it is time for the mazurka and the waltz. So, gentle reader, read on.

Sir Reresby Sitwell, Bt, London, 2000.

viii

There will be a ball in the Winter Palace to‑
night.

We invite any who would see St. Peters‑
burg in its snow and gilt to spend the day with us.
And, later, climb the great stair and be lost in an
enchanted world which, we are told, should not
have been. None the less, there will be the ball to‑
night. We will see the flowers and uniforms, and
hear the mazurka and the waltz. This very day that
the snowflakes are falling. And, while they fall,
Alexander II is Tsar. It is, at present, a winter
morning early in 1868.

We choose that year because we would have it in
a time of peace before the Russo‑Turkish war, and
in the era of the crinoline before Sedan. The Nihi‑
lists are not yet busy in the capital. And, for our
purposes, we prefer this Tsar to his successor Alex‑
ander III, who cared little for ceremony. With
Alexander II we touch the Russia of Nicholas I,
his father. Much of what we will see has changed
but little since the time of that Tsar's father, the

mad Paul I, and has come down unaltered from the reign of Catherine the Great. So we will let it be. It is a January morning in 1868. The writer, or, if you like, the reader, is to be a disembodied guest who sees and is not seen, who goes everywhere. If this is agreed, we will worry no more about the classic unities, the conventions of when, and how, and where, but begin straightway.

Already, the Court runner has come round. A peculiarly dressed individual out of a pantomime or ballet who got down from a carriage, a messenger, a running footman, a skorokhod; as rare a being as a heyduck or an eunuch, only surviving, indeed, at the Russian court, and sent out on the morning of a ball to take the invitations. He has to drive in a car-riage because the capital is too big for him to go on foot. It is a first taste of the world of artifice into which we are about to enter; but he came early in the morning and we did not see him. Tonight, the whole corps of skorokhods will be on duty. We leave their strange uniform till then, and are awake and breakfasting in a foreign Embassy, a private palace, or even the Winter Palace itself, any or all of them, as suits our purpose. And the snow is no longer falling. There is the typical pale green nor-

thern sky of winter, while below, sledges innumer‑
able are drawn rapidly and noiselessly over the snow.

We will go for our luncheon to a restaurant, for
the late morning has slipped by, doing nothing, and
smoking long‑tipped, yellow cigarettes. To Donon
or Cubat: it does not matter which. This is to be a
holiday for the writer and, we hope, the reader, too.
Cubat, in point of accuracy, is not opened yet. It
belongs to the 'eighties, the period of Alexander III;
but Donon and Cubat are the famous restaurants of
the capital, and in the food we order the national
character will begin. First of all in the zakuska, or
hors d'œuvres. Fresh caviar; balik (sturgeon dried
in the sun); raw smoked goose; and twenty, thirty,
forty other things. With these we drink a glass of
allasch (kümmel), or of listofka, which is flavoured
with the young leaves of the black currant. If feeling
rich—and why not in St. Petersburg, in 1868!—we
could follow this with sterlet soup from the Volga,
which may cost as much as ten shillings a person;
but we are content with riabchik, a kind of grouse
or partridge, and as tender as its name. To drink
with this there could be nothing more delicious,
even on a winter day, than malinovoi, or raspberry
kvas. And, now, we can begin to wander.

## A CRINOLINE IN THE CORRIDOR

Perhaps the first sensation of Russia came in the Russian train. After passports had been scrutinized at the frontier, and every bit of luggage, every book and letter looked at separately. But into the train, at last. It consists of half a dozen waggons of immense length. An Englishman who came here a couple of years ago, 1866, for the marriage of the Tsarewitch, describes it with enthusiasm.

Entering by the middle you come into a small saloon with a table in the centre surrounded by sofas and divans. From one side of this saloon a passage, broad and high enough for a tall man or a lady in a crinoline to walk along without difficulty, leads into the private compartments. On the roof there is a sleeping saloon, to which you ascend by a winding stairway. Lamps are lit, the curtains drawn, a green baize table is fixed into the centre of the floor, wax candles are fastened at the corners. And presently, the train stops at a brilliantly lit station, with hand/ some arcades. Snow is falling. But there is half an hour for dinner. On one side is the samovar, in such contrast to the ham sandwich and the English pot of tea! Ducks and geese and venison, huge fishes and plump partridges, galantines, jellies and pud/ dings; soups and joints for those who prefer hot meat to cold; stacks of bottles of French wines; and decanters of native liqueurs. The waiters, like those at Donon's, are dressed in long red linen coats. There is an icon on the wall. Peasant women offer slippers and embroidered scarves for sale. An old priest, with a white beard, walks up and down holding a gilt plate, on which you throw a kopeck. It is holy Russia. Russia of the starving and the millionaire! That was only yesterday. And it is still strange today.

In St. Petersburg. But the very air has character out of the immense open spaces. In what other town in the world could the fronts of three buildings only, of painted stucco, set end to end, be two-thirds of a mile in length! One building alone, the famous Admiralty, of which we know the spire from the backcloth in *Petrouchka*, has a main façade four hundred and fifty yards long, while the side wings running down to the Neva are more than two hundred yards in extent. So much for officialdom, or bureaucracy. It has, at least, walls of gay colours and a gilded spire. More than this, the painted stucco is designed specially to look bright against the snow. We will return to that later. Character is more than plaster architecture. It can be built up out of words and cadences.

## GYPSY MUSIC

A Gypsy band is playing and the music, which is Russian with something added of their own, makes a wonderful vehicle in which to wander, a sledge or traineau, we could call it, sometimes slow, and again, furious and headlong, while we think of many things and, in effect, come up to them and see them with our eyes. All the time we hear phrases of the music so that, from now on, we breathe and taste and smell the Russian air. Not forgetting why we came here. In preparation for the fairy tale extravagance of where we go tonight. Wealth and luxury beyond belief, such as the world has seldom seen, while the snow falls outside, and in cellars, men who are sunk to the level of brutes and women all in rags, neither men nor women looking any more like human beings, all filthy, drink together at long deal tables, literally black with dirt. These contrasts: and little in between. Nothing that need bother us, for our subject is the two extremes.

Did you hear that? Listen to the shape of it! It must have come out of some low tavern. It has a fiery spirit in it. A drunken song. But not altogether. It is music which is loyal but, in the end, will not forgive. A brutal force which falls in its own way. But, in its own moment, generous and inspired.

And they play another tune which is sentimental and nostalgic, speaking of the troika and the birch trees. We see the pale green sky of winter, like that the high gilt needle of the Admiralty pricks into. For it brings us back into the town. For a moment, in imagination, we are in its open spaces in front of the Cathedral of St. Isaac, contemplating its granite monoliths dug out of the swamps of Finland; its pillars of lapis lazuli at the entrance; and the columns of malachite at the altar; but we need not enter. The mere sketch or impression is enough. Holy Russia does not interest us, at this moment.

Instead, we would sooner find ourselves in the Summer Garden, which is full of nursemaids and governesses, and little children dressed à la moujik, a year or two, precisely, after the liberation of the serfs. An Englishman who came to St. Petersburg thirty years earlier, in 1838, was witness of a curious scene which, somehow, connects itself with the sight of these children playing in the Summer Garden. 'Opposite to the Admiralty, in the open place, large wooden booths had been erected for theatrical and other exhibitions, and in front of the booths were what are called Katchellies, namely, swings and merry-go-rounds. On the three last days there was a carriage promenade in front of the Katchellies; and in the throng a string of twenty coaches-and-six, followed by six outriders, was conspicuous. The carriages were plain and neat, painted green, and all exactly alike, with handsome powerful horses, equipped in heavy German harness, and the coachmen, postillions, footmen, and outriders, dressed in scarlet great coats with capes, cocked hats, leather breeches, and jack boots. These were court equipages, and each carriage contained six young ladies belonging to the public institutions or schools at St. Petersburg under the patronage of the Tsarina, who annually bestows this indulgence upon the pupils.' [1] This annual custom was abolished when that Empress died, but the proof that it had been is the St. Petersburg we want. We are, immediately, in the reign of Nicholas I. And, indeed, our whole purpose is to see that, and the time of Catherine the Great, from a fixed point in the reign of Alexander II.

Many of these young girls will have come from the Smolny convent, or Institution des Demoiselles

[1] Alexandra Feodorowna, wife of Nicholas I, a princess of Wurtemburg.

Nobles, a beautiful rococo building with a high belfry, by Count Rastrelli, a name with which we must become familiar, for he was architect, originally, both of the Winter Palace and Tsarskoe Selo. But that, also, is a matter that can stand. The picture of those young girls driving in Court carriages past the swings and merry-go-rounds, and of the nurses and governesses, and children dressed as moujiks, is more Russian than the Venetian, Count Rastrelli. How wonderful the popular music will have been! We hear the hurdygurdy and the organ, fanfares on bugles, and the rolling of a drum. That is after Easter, every year. But now, the open place is empty. But not of persons. There is a crowd of people hurrying to and fro, nearly every man in uniform, but most of them officials with a satchel in their hands. Even the poorest may wear a military cap, the relic of their conscript days, which, with their round and bearded heads, their high cheek bones and their hair falling over their faces just like thatch, makes them resemble the waxwork figure of—is it Burke or Hare?—at Madame Tussaud's. And, of course, there are the droshky, or rather, sledge drivers, in long blue caftans and black, low-crowned hats, bearded like the rest, but more robust, for, at least, they earn a living and do not walk the streets and crowd the cellars.

We may fancy we hear in all this the ghosts of music of the fair. The wheezing organ, the bugle and the drum. But come back to the Summer Garden! There could be no better place in which to resume the capital and get its feeling. It runs beside the Neva. The first scene of *Pique Dame*, Tchaikowsky's opera to a play by Pushkin, is laid in the Summer Garden with a chorus of nursemaids and governesses and young men of the capital, who are taking the spring air. And it follows our pattern. In the second act there is a ball.

But we will read on. 'The last and gayest of the promenades took place the day before yesterday. It was attended by the court, and all the fashionable world. Every vehicle in St. Petersburg was placed in requisition. All the carriages were obliged to pass down our street, in order to enter the Admiralty place. Soon after six o'clock, the officers of the regiment of Gardes à cheval, who had been gradually assembling, drew up under our windows in scarlet uniforms, waiting to escort the Emperor, who in the course of half an hour drove up in a plain open carriage with a pair of horses, accompanied by his eldest son. They stopped opposite to us, threw off their cloaks, and appeared in the same uniform as the officers in attendance; an aide-de-camp brought the Emperor his horse, which he mounted, and his son following his example, he saluted right and left, and rode on, followed by the Gardes à cheval. As they disappeared under the arch of the État Major, the Empress with her three daughters turned into the street, at the other end, and passed down it in a handsome open carriage-and-four, with two postillions, in blue-and-silver jackets, and velvet caps, and escorted by a party of officers of the Chevaliers Gardes.'

The Gardes à cheval and their rivals, the Chevaliers Gardes! But perhaps the mind and physiognomy of Nicholas I, for it was he, are apparent in his favourite uniform. He was continually portrayed in this; whether by the English portrait painter Dawe, who spent his life at the Russian court, or in other paintings, and even upon porcelain from the Imperial manufactory. To these resplendent uniforms of the Chevaliers Gardes and the Gardes à cheval there attaches more than a little interest. It would take a better military historian than the present writer to decide which was the first of the sovereigns of Europe, after the Napoleonic wars, to put his heavy cavalry, or personal bodyguard, into breastplates of polished steel. Nothing of the kind had been worn since the wars of Louis XIV, and they were an anachronism, then. It may have been the sartorial genius of the Prince Regent, but the proposal was sanctioned by the Duke of Wellington, and the necessary armourers' shops fitted up and set to work. This readiness to embark upon so novel and original an idea makes it likely that it was no invention but a copy of some fashion from abroad. None of the Garde Impériale of Napoleon wore breastplates. We would suggest, therefore, that it came from Russia.

The question forms a curious chapter in the history of taste. What was the intention? That they were mediaeval paladins, or heroes from the Trojan wars? Russia is no land of Gothic, and this may have been the Muscovite attempt at that. In the result, these armoured horsemen are the grafting of mediaevalism, of the sham Gothic of 1820, upon the classicism of the time. They form a hybrid, but one which, like many crossbreedings, had an individuality of its own. Later accounts of ceremonies in Russia often speak of these two regiments, with the

gold or silver double eagles in their helms, as Wag-
nerian knights, but this, again, argues a change of
taste. The details of the uniforms, too, had been
slightly modified by then. Our argument is that it
was a Russian whim and one of the typical extra-
vagancies of Russian luxury. In the early years of
Nicholas I the Chevalier Gardes wore the black
crested horsetail helms, like those of our Life Guards
of the day, but these were soon altered to the eagle
helm, about the same time that the uniform of our
Life Guard and Horse Guards Blue took on the
modified form we know.

It is idle, but interesting, to calculate the population of armoured horsemen in mid-nineteenth century Europe. Two British regiments: two Russian:
two similar regiments in the Prussian Guard: the
Pope's Guardia Nobile: the Sardinian Guardia
del Re: the Cuirassiers and Cent Gardes of Napoleon III: the total is considerable, but we hope to
have proved that it was Russian by invention. Alexander may have begun it: but it was Nicholas, the
autocrat or oligarch, who made it usual and fixed
the type.

Nicholas I, to whom the aspect of the capital is
due. It reflects his classical and precise mind, the

most perfect of autocrats there has ever been. In some ways, as historians have said, more remarkable than any ruler of his time. But it needed more than Nicholas to give character to the town. His architects, who were Russian for the first time, designed the classical façades, with the difference of the bright colours they were painted, while the ultra-conservatism of the Tsar imprisoned, as it were, the national characteristics and passed them on. Nicholas, we would remind ourselves, was third son of the mad Paul I. Born in 1796, in the year that Catherine died, he took no part in politics during the reign of his eldest brother, Alexander I, but was occupied entirely with his military duties. When Alexander died mysteriously at Taganrog in Southern Russia, in 1825, it was supposed that his second brother, Constantine, would succeed him. Did Alexander really die; or was his journey with its curious circumstances to a remote part of his dominions a ruse by which he sought to disappear from the world? It is well known that his tomb in St. Petersburg is empty. We will not enter, here, into conjecture, one way or the other. Some say that he retired to Mount Athos; or into a convent in the Holy Land. Another story is that an aged hermit, who in some obscure way was protected by authority, and who used to ramble of the great personages he had known half a century before, was the Tsar Alexander I. If it was Alexander, he died as the staretz Theodore Kousmitch, near Tomsk in Siberia, in February 1864. All this may have been in order that he should expiate his connivance in the murder of his father, Paul I, in 1801.

On the death of Alexander, for this must be assumed in history, Constantine did not succeed him. He had signed a document abdicating all his claims. This prince, who was sixteen years older than Nicholas, born in the full glory of the reign of Catherine the Great, had been given a name intended to be prophetic of his destiny. Alexander, the eldest brother, would be Tsar; Constantine, the restored Basileus of a Byzantine Empire. The favourite Potemkin, who had conquered the Crimea and the Chersonese, and been created Prince of the Tauride, was destined for a kingdom of Dacia, compound of Wallachia and Moldavia. Such were the schemes of Catherine the Great. But we return to 1825. On the death of his brother, Constantine, as we have said, renounced the Russian throne, and retired with his Polish wife to his command at Warsaw. Nicholas I became Tsar; and had immediately to quell a military insurrection. We need only add, for historical completion, that he reigned till 1855 and died, broken hearted, during the Crimean War, being succeeded by his son, Alexander II.

Nicholas was handsome, like Alexander I, and of the great height that was conspicuous in the Romanov family up to Nicholas II, and indeed in most of the figures in Russian history until Stalin and Lenin are reached. The Marquis de Custine says of him: 'Un tel homme ne peut être jugé d'après la mesure qu'on applique aux hommes ordinaires . . . son front superbe, ses traits qui tiennent de l'Apollon et de Jupiter.' Another writer remarks of Nicholas that his personal grandeur of stature and aspect was beyond description. He added to his classical features, noticed by all contemporaries, by dressing his hair with Macassar oil, after the manner of an antique bust. His favourite uniform, we note, was that of the Gardes à cheval, one of the two regiments of Horse Guards to whom we were introduced by the English traveller, a moment or two ago. And, as though to bring that paragraph to life, in a square behind the Admiralty there stands

SOLDIERS, OR PARTERRES OF TULIPS?
the equestrian statue of Nicholas in the uniform of
the Horse Guards, upon a pedestal of granite, while
the four emblematic figures at the corners are cast
from the features of the Tsarina and her three
daughters, whom we saw driving past the Admiralty in a handsome open carriage. Of his military
tastes there is much in evidence. In the Alexander
Palace, built by Catherine for her grandson Alexander in the park at Tsarskoe Selo, but a favourite
residence of Nicholas, there are glass cases contain-
ing models of the different regiments of cavalry,
carried out, as to man and horse, with utmost
accuracy and beauty. Other rooms have military
pictures of soldiers in stiff squares, like parterres,
works of that German or Viennese school of the
'thirties and 'forties which, in its naïveté, is about the
last unexplored province in the continent of painting. Bright sunshine, as of a day in early spring,
hides no detail of those wooden figures.

Walking on a little further you would find,
strange ghosts, a Chinese village of twenty-four
houses perched on artificial rocks or scrolls, their
eaves hung with bells, inhabited by gardeners and
their families, with Chinese bridges criss-crossing a
canal; a Chinese tower with a high pole in front of

it rigged like the mast of a frigate; a Gothic building called the Admiralty; a Dutch and a Swiss dairy; a Turkish kiosque; a summer house in the form of an Ionic colonnade supporting a hanging garden (this building is by Charles Cameron and the Emperor often dined here in the summer); triumphal arches; rostral columns; a pavilion where the Grand Duchesses used to feed their swans; a lake with a fleet of pygmy boats of all descriptions manned by sailors of the Imperial Guard—and, not yet, the Palace. But traces, at least, of the six hundred gar⁄deners.

What is there particularly Russian in all this? The Chinese village; the rostral column; the feeding of the swans. And we may even think we know three generations in the succession of these words. As to the Chinese village, no one but an Elizabeth or a Catherine would have been fanciful upon such a scale as this. It is in the taste, at least, of Elizabeth. The rostral column, on the other hand, is typical of Catherine. And we get, in this, the difference in their two reigns. China, with its land connection through distant Siberia to Russia, means another thing to Russians to what it does with us. If Great Britain was connected by land with India, however many thousand miles away, we would have another conception of that land of elephant and tiger in the knowledge that waves of invasion had come to us direct from India, itself, and that, in proverb, we were partly Indian in origin.

Was not part of Moscow, in the centre of that city, called the Kitai Gorod, or Chinese Town? It was a mere name, having nothing celestial about it, unless the cathedral of St. Basil, with its many domes, each of different colour and design, is so fantastic that it could be called Chinese. The beginning of China was the land's end of Russia, reached by horse, or upon foot, but not by sea. Upon state occasions the Empress Elizabeth was preceded in her gilded coach by two horsemen of her bodyguard, one a Chinese cavalier, and the other wearing European armour and mounted on a Kirghiz horse. This afternoon, in January 1868, and perhaps now, we could go to the Museum of Imperial carriages and see some carnival sledges of fantastic form. One is a group of the dragon and St. George; another has a seat like a peepshow box carried by a showman. A figure in the dress of a harlequin is placed in the front; and another, in the costume of a Levantine, between him and the driver. We would see phaetons, calèches, and vis-a-vis, some of them with painted panels by Gravelot or Boucher, the travel-ling and town equipages on the lower floor, and gala coaches and carriages upstairs. We would be shown, too, if in the mood, the gilded harness for the horses, and state liveries for eight hundred men. Downstairs, in the Imperial Stables, are three hun-dred horses and half that number more for saddle horses.

We have said that the rostral column was charac-teristic of Catherine the Great. She began her reign in the prevailing taste of the Empress Elizabeth, her mother-in-law, daughter of the Tsar Peter and, like her father, giant and barbarian in her life and works. But Catherine was only Russian by adoption, though, like many converts, that much more genuine in the faith she had embraced. Rastrelli, or his contemporaries, belonged to an older generation, or were dead. Catherine employed, as architects, Quarenghi or Cameron, and her buildings and their details were classical in the Russian manner. Trophies, triumphal arches, rostral columns, were her rage. The pavilion where the Grand Duchesses came to feed their swans, if we add to it a weeping willow, needs no further signature of reign or time.

## FAÇADE STAINED IN THREE COLOURS

It belongs to an epoch when music and poetry were written, but the other arts were dead. Not so long ago, for remember this is 1868!

Now we are at Tsarskoe Selo we should, at least, come up to the empty palace, for it is winter, and look through the gilded windows. An earlier tra⁄veller, whom we may envy, left the capital at sun⁄rise and came here by sledge. All round, in every direction, there are pavilions and little palaces by Charles Cameron, Quarenghi, Menelas and Rossi; but come nearer! A façade, twelve hundred feet in length, and stained green and white and yellow, climbs out of the snow. It has three storeys. The front is broken by three advancing portions, and in the middle section we can count three rows of fifteen windows. The other two advancing portions, to right and left, contain one hundred large windows, in each direction, divided by caryatids upon the ground floor, and by detached Corinthian columns and pilasters on the first storey and the attic. The roof is crowded with statues and with vases. Once, every statue, every pedestal, every capital, all the vases and ornaments, were gilt. Now, they are stained yellow. The roof is gabled, like that of the Tuileries. In front of this façade there are two long semi-circular wings. On the garden side, the other front of the palace is less ornamented and gives on to a terrace and a parterre. The gardens extend in that direction for at least four miles. Internally, the whole of this immense line of building forms but one un-interrupted suite of rooms, upon two floors, and in double or parallel lines, the projecting portions of the front being intended only to give greater scale to the more important of the state apartments.

Rastrelli was architect of this fantastic building. Its peculiar note is struck at the outset by the colour-ing of the external walls, a concession to barbarian taste, which was not content with brick or stone. The special purpose was against the monotony of snow, but it is as Russian in invention as the cathe-dral of St. Basil and its coloured domes. From this are descended the painted façades of the Admiralty and of so many buildings in St. Petersburg of the time of Nicholas I. This hybrid Italian has become the vernacular of Russia; of foreign instigation, but as typical of Russia as the Russian cuisine or the classical ballets of Petipa.

The builder of Tsarskoe Selo was the Empress Elizabeth. Many of the rooms are in the rococo of her period, with the Russian flavour. A profusion of gilding, barbarian in its extravagance, doors and ceilings that are beautiful and splendid. A room of which the entire panelling is formed of amber, in homage to the Baltic and its sandy shores;[1] and a hall of lapis lazuli with a parquet of ebony inlaid with wreaths of mother-of-pearl. A change in taste came with the arrival of Charles Cameron, an architect who was recommended to Catherine by his publication of a book of measured drawings of classical remains, another Adam, or James Wyatt, a reputed Jacobite, but little or nothing is yet known of him. At his first coming he was set to work by Catherine with the simplest materials. The bedroom of the Empress is often quoted because of its walls of porcelain and pilasters of violet glass. These latter are no more than panels of glass laid over velvet of that colour, due, probably, to a sketch or a mere suggestion from Cameron and appealing to Catherine because of its cleverness and as a joke or comment upon the extravagance of her other schemes. Later, he was allowed more expensive materials and, in addition to building, designed furniture of all descriptions and details that were as fine as jewellers'

[1] The amber was presented by Frederick the Great to the Empress Anna Ivanovna (1730–1740).

or goldsmiths' work. It can only be presumed that he found, ready for him, whole studios of craftsmen in their different branches. The Italian Quarenghi was his contemporary, working in an orthodox Palladian style, somehow acclimatized to St. Petersʹ burg. He was more purely an architect, not a forʹ gotten genius like Cameron, but an Italian who returned home to die, well known and eulogized in Bergamo, his native town. Cameron worked extensively at Pavlovsk, too, where the colonnade must be his masterpiece. Much of his furniture reʹ mains in these two palaces, chairs and settees being upholstered with Lyons silk woven specially for the barbarian North by Philippe Lassalle and other craftsmen, with such patterns, in one instance, as a design of silver and gold pheasants, bright as new. Every technical intricacy of process is employed upon these silks and, perhaps, none but the court of Russia would have countenanced their cost.

What we would have of Tsarskoe Selo, or the other palaces, is no more details but a confusion of their charms. The sensation of sleeping on a summer night with this fantastic world around one. Or their haunted loneliness upon a winter day; today, for instance, when the Court is in St. Petersburg and preparing for the ball tonight. What of Gatchina, or Oranienbaum, of Pavlovsk, Peterhof, or the many smaller palaces? There is no time for these. Whom would we prefer to see? Zoritch, the favourite of Catherine, by birth a Croat or a Bosnian, in his hussar uniform of scarlet and silver, ablaze with diamond orders? One or other of the prime favourites in their day, or on their night, of splendour?[1] But we will not be drawn from one century into another.

We would sooner attend a military review. In the camp at Krasnoe Selo: or in the Champ de Mars: it does not matter which. At Krasnoe Selo the Tsar reviews the Imperial Guard in August and the Tsarina and her ladies attend in white dresses with white bouquets in their hands. She arrives on the parade ground in a calèche drawn by eight albino horses with pink eyes. At the Champ de Mars it could be this afternoon, or any other day. For we

[1] The brothers Orlov, Vissensky, Vassiltschikev, Potemkin, Zavadovsky, Zoritch, Rimsky-Korsakov, Lanskoi, Yermolov, Momonov, Plato and Valerian Zubov, received in money alone, from the hands of Catherine, some ninety million roubles, which was the equivalent of fifteen million pounds in mid-Victorian England. In our time it could not be calculated. In addition, they received other gifts, houses, and huge estates with tens of thousands of serfs attached.

BANDS ALONG THE GRANITE QUAYS
come back again and again to the capital, and every
moment away from it is time lost of our few hours
before the ball tonight. Because of that, as on other
festivals, there is, most certainly, a review today. Now,
at this moment, before it grows dark at half-past
three. In the Champ de Mars, beside the Neva and
the Summer Garden, watched by the children's
nurses in their high kokoshniks. But why not in the
great square, in front of the Winter Palace? Here,
reviews were held while the Emperors dared risk
assassination.

We hear bands of military music marching to the
parade along the granite quays, coming from the
barracks of the Preobrajenski regiment. Soon, martial music can be heard from other directions, giving
an indescribable excitement to this winter afternoon.
Forty thousand men of the Russian Imperial Guard
are to be reviewed. Salvos of guns are firing from
the fortress of St. Peter and St. Paul, across the Neva.
We reach the square in time to see the troops con-
verging and high officers arrive, some in sledges
drawn by splendid horses, others in closed carriages
along the snow. On alighting, they throw off their
cloaks, exhibiting rows of ribbons, stars and decora-
tions, over uniforms of green, and white, and scarlet.

## A PERSIAN TRIUMPH

The regiment of the Chevaliers Gardes rides forth at this moment from the portico of their Manège or riding school, which is a classical building by Quar⁄ enghi, mounted on bay horses, dressed in their white uniforms, with black horsetail helmets and cui⁄ rasses, carrying the Persian standards,[1] and preceded by an entire band of trumpeters. They proceed at the peculiar slowness of a horse's walking pace, and take up their station. Opposite to them, the Gardes à cheval in scarlet uniforms are assembling.

The Tsar, who rides out from the central archway of the palace with a great suite of officers in attend⁄ ance, is received with three tremendous roulades of

[1] From the Persian war of 1828. The Russian ambassador Griboyedov was murdered in Teheran. On the conclusion of peace, the Persian gifts consisted of a long train of rare animals, Persian webs, gold stuffs, and pearls. They reached St. Petersburg in winter. The pearls and gold stuffs and rich shawls were carried in great silver and gold dishes by magni⁄ ficently dressed Persians. The Persian Prince Khosreff Mirza drove in an Imperial State equipage with six horses; the ele⁄ phants, bearing on their backs towers filled with Indian warriors, had leathern boots to protect them from the cold, and the cages of the lions and tigers were provided with double skins of the northern polar bears. The greater part of this tribute of pearls was given to the monastery of St. Alex⁄ ander Nevski, at the end of the Nevski Prospekt, where it was used to ornament mitres and rich vestments.

the trumpets and the drums. The drums beat again while he gallops down the line, his horse being already covered with foam. He then mounts a fresh charger and rides through the ranks by the side of the Tsarina's carriage-and-four which, after this, is drawn up before the centre of the line. The band of each regiment stations itself opposite the Emperor, and the march past begins. The curiosity of this performance is that you hear the Tsar's voice as each battalion goes past. He makes some remark to them: 'Well marched', or 'Very good', and the entire battalion shouts a reply. The cavalry come first, preceded only by the Tsar's personal bodyguard, mounted Circassians or Mamelukes of the Guard, some armed with carbines and some with bows and arrows. Scarlet or white predominate in their uniform, but each is dressed according to the fashion of his country. They are divided into Leszghines or Tcherkesses, in respect of Circassia or the Transcaucasus, and are all Circassian gentlemen or native princes, including, now, two sons of the famous Schamyl, in white caftans and golden belts with high white lambskin caps.

The Gardes à cheval and the Chevalier Gardes come next: huge men, picked for their height: the

## RUSSIAN IMPERIAL HYMN

Gardes à cheval in immense jack-boots and helmets that sparkle like steel, surmounted by double-headed gilded eagles, their gilt breastplates fastened over their snow-white tunics. As each battalion, marching past, comes to the salute, its regimental band immediately opposite the Tsar, bursts afresh into a frenzied rendering of the Russian national anthem, Boje Tsar chrani. This tune was composed for Nicholas I by Prince Lwow. Apart from the Marseillaise, there is no patriotic air that is so stirring and none that, in a few bars, paints a whole country and a people. In this, it is equal to the immortal Glinka. The reiteration of this noble anthem, twenty or thirty times over, each time with different instruments, never twice alike, thrills and intoxicates like nothing else. It is the expression of this nation of eighty million persons. Unlike the Marseillaise, this tune does not flag towards the middle; and we could contrast the recovery of that, with its 'aux armes' of fanfares and of trumpets, to its magnificent peroration, with the clashing and maddened cymbals breaking in, half way through, and carrying this other intoxication to its triumphant end. That it is a sort of drug or stimulant given to the troops as they come past, no one can doubt. It bursts forth, again

and again, with sublime effect, and that clension or
stroke of genius towards the end. No one who saw
a military review in the old Imperial days can ever
forget this.

After the Horse Guards come four regiments
of Cuirassiers, a portion of each regiment being
equipped as Lancers. Their bands, like all cavalry
bands, are shrill and high. These four regiments are
distinguished by their different colourings and facings: black breastplates, or steel breastplates: tunics
that are blue or red, or green or white. After them,
a superb train of Horse Artillery, drawing field guns
that shine like telescopes or steel instruments, the
caissons painted a light green colour, and a pair of
soldiers seated, back to back, on each. But, in the
impossibility of giving each regiment enough atten-
tion as it goes past, we discuss them statically, as
though they stood quite still. In this manner we
come to the regiment of Horse Grenadiers, mounted
on white horses, and have time to consider this
anomaly. For a few years in the reign of George IV
our own regiment of the Horse Guards Blue wore
steel breastplates, and not a helm, but a huge bearskin of immense height, and great gauntlets and
swords of exaggerated length, like those of an

imaginary Crusader. This costume, if striking, must have been most cumbersome, to judge from contemporary engravings. In fact, it was so awkward that it was soon discontinued. The bearskin is, of course, entirely Russian in conception. But this subvariety, for we are led to speak of these freaks of militarism as though they were curious flowers or birds, had an echo in Belgium, as well, where part of the Royal Grenadiers were mounted, in the reigns of Leopold I and Leopold II. They were allowed to lapse, in time. However, just before the present war, when King Leopold III drove in state to the opening of the exhibition in Liège, he was escorted by Horse Grenadiers, the last date, we may be certain, of their appearance in the modern world. The grenadier is so typically an infantryman that it is peculiar to see him mounted; but their military band, at least, has heavy brass instruments and not merely bugles and trumpets and kettledrums, while the sappers of this regiment, who are bearded giants, beside the red trousers, blue tunics and red epaulettes, wear the long white leather aprons of their office and carry the pickaxe and the shovel.

There are Hussars of the Guard, in scarlet uniforms and mounted upon greys, a Hungarian invention of the eighteenth century, in descent from the Pandours and irregular levies of the Turkish frontier, the hussar uniform, indeed, being an adap-tation, conscious or unconscious, of the Magyar peasant costume. The Hungarian magnates had their heyducks, or bodyguards, dressed like that. After the hussar regiments were formed by Charles VI and Maria Theresa, the custom spread all over Europe, and to Russia.[1]

In the eighteenth century no other body of men wore whiskers or moustaches. For this, alone, they were conspicuous in an age of powdered hair. The cult of the hussar was at its height in Germany, of which the Black Brunswickers or Death's Head Hussars are an example; while, during the reign of Frederick the Great, there were twenty-five hussar regiments in the Prussian army, more than one con-

[1] The Hungarian Life Guard must have been the ne plus ultra of the hussar. They wore a scarlet hussar uniform en-riched with silver lace, a tiger skin pellisse, high yellow boots, and a high fur cap surmounted by a heron's plume, while their grey horses had green housings and silver bridles. This corps was founded by Maria Theresa, and only dis-banded in November 1918. They were quartered in Vienna, in a palace designed by Fischer von Erlach; while their colonel became, on appointment, a Baron of the Holy Roman Empire.

temporary work upon military costume being given up to the minute delineation of their differences in colour, their dolmans or slung jackets, and their exceptionally high, cylindrical, hussar caps, a detail which was characteristic of that time, but had be/come much shortened by 1868. Here before us, in the square of the Winter Palace, we have three hussar regiments; the scarlet, whom we mentioned, whose officers have silver facings to their uniforms, and two others. One of them is the Heir Apparent's own regiment, led by the giant Tsarewitch in person; white hussars, in white dolmans with gold facings. This prince, six foot five inches tall and strong in proportion, the future Alexander III, who became Tsar upon the assassination of his father in 1881, was last of the huge Romanovs.[1] It is pro/bably true to say that it was the physical height and strength of these giant men, from Alexander I, that supported the Russian monarchy through the nine/

[1] The Tsarewitch had married, in 1866, the Danish prin/cess, Dagmar, afterwards the Tsarina Marie/Feodorovna, and sister of Queen Alexandra. The last of the Romanov family in whom the great stature was conspicuous was the Grand Duke Nicholas/Nicolaievitch, Russian Comman/der/in/chief during the last war, who was a grandson of Nicholas I.

41

teenth century until the accession of the puny
Nicholas II. This Tsarewitch, from his tremendous
stature, made a great impression on all who saw him.
Igor Strawinsky describes him, in an open letter
discussing the *Sleeping Beauty* of Tchaikowsky:
'In the first place it is a personal joy, for this work
appears to me as the most authentic expression of
that period of Russian life which we call the Petersburg period, and which is stamped upon my memory
with the moving vision of the Imperial sleighs of
Alexander III, the Giant Emperor and his giant
coachman. . . .' This is the Tsarewitch whom we
see marching past at the head of his own regiment of white hussars. They are followed by dra-
goons of Sversk and Pereiaslav, and by a regiment
of Uhlans or lancers in red uniforms, wearing the
lancer's cap or czapska, which is in sign of Polish
origin.

So much for the cavalry. The infantry are, mostly,
grey coated, as in the Crimean war, and wear the
bachlik, one of the typical features of Russian costume, worn, even, by the ancient Scythians, as can
be seen on the silver vases in the Hermitage, a grey
hood with tails crossed upon the breast like belts,
and put over the head at night in the snow and

wind of a Russian winter. Several regiments of
grenadiers come first, the leading company of each
breaking into a hoarse cheer as it passes by the Tsar.
It is not good marching: not to be compared to our
Brigade of Guards, but has a servile, grey monotony
and the sense of limitless numbers, if needed, for
the slaughter. Another regiment runs past, at the
double; but, in all the regiments of grenadiers, so
difficult to know one from another, there is, to the
foreigner, something typically Russian in the shaggy
shape of their bearskins, and in the knowledge that
this is, particularly, a Russian invention, coming,
we would suppose, from the first bear hunters in the
Urals. There are the Guards of Finland, who are
light infantry or tirailleurs; and the Lithuanian and
Volhynian Guard, in the képis of the rifleman or
chasseurs à pied, in uniforms of shadowy blue as
though for fighting in their native woods. Some of
the finer infantry are kept till last. They are the Preobrajenski, or regiment of the Transfiguration; a
Praetorian Guard of grenadiers for they have the
right of entry, at all times, into the Winter Palace.
These bearded men have the look of veterans of 1812.
Last of all come the Pavlovski, one of the oddest of
the freaks of militarism, for they are a snub-nosed

regiment, founded by the mad Paul I, and confined
to those who reproduced his Kalmuck features.
Moreover, of all regiments in the Russian army, they
alone still wore the hat, like a half sugar loaf, of the
Russian grenadiers of the time of Frederick William
I, before the bearskin became the fashion, this hat
being of copper, embossed in front with the Russian
double eagle, and absolutely of another century in
type and style. It is easy, in seeing them, to picture
the dreadful military punishment in the Russian
army of running the gauntlet, or passing between the
halberds, as it was called in mitigation. They pass
by with a hoarse roar, and a curious hollow sound
upon the snow, to the dying notes of their tremendous martial band.

The review ends with a furious charge of Cossacks, the square being nearly empty, for the other
troops had marched to their different barracks. It is
led by the Cossacks of the Guard in their scarlet
caftans brandishing their swords, which, with the
curved blades, flash like silver. The officers of the
Cossack Guard, could we note them in detail, have
golden belts and bandoliers. No other Cossacks
take part, except the Ataman Cossacks, in sapphire
blue uniforms, who are one of the crack regiments of

Russia.[1] They are the special regiment of the Tsarewitch, for both Alexander II, and the future Alexander III, wore the dress of Cossack Ataman at
every opportunity, as Nicholas I favoured that of the
Gardes à cheval. Alexander III, in fact, was *en
cosaque* all his life. The fantasia ends with a
flourish and a fusillade; and when the last squadron
has gone by the Tsar turns his horse, and with the
Tsarewitch following him, rides slowly off the
square, under the great archway of the Winter
Palace. Once more the snow has begun to fall.

This extraordinary city sparkles, now, with a
myriad lights. They have not waited for the winter sun
to set. The display of military pomp and pageantry
we have just witnessed could be an hallucination,
were it not that, as we walk away, the façade of the
Winter Palace stretches for nearly half a mile along
the Neva, that frozen river, till we reach the still
vaster Admiralty, and passing under the tropheal

[1] There were, in fact, in the Russian army, Cossacks of the
Don, the Caucasus, of Astrakhan, the Sea of Azov, the
Black Sea, Orenburg, the Ural, of Mestcherak (Bashkirs),
and, as well, of Siberia and the trans-Baikal, who guarded
the frontier towards China. The uniform of most of these
was the dull Cossack green. The Tsar was Ataman of all
the Cossacks.

arch of the État Major, third of these gigantic build<i>
ings, turn a corner, and are in a moment in the
Nevski Prospekt. At this point the shops have not
begun. From afar, once again, come the sounds of a
military band. But they have no connection, any
more, with actuality: they are intangible forms, wild
strange fancies, built up, none the less, from solid
fact, for they are snatches of martial music, real or
imaginary. What happens to the poor in this enor<i>
mous city? It is the town of Dives and Lazarus: of
palaces and filthy cellars. Not a face, in those, that
was not bleared and blotched and blurred by drink.
The walls are slimy wet with breath. Men and
women are huddled together on the wooden ben<i>
ches. There are degrees, descending steps of poverty,
even here. If you would have a hideous vision, look
lower, upon a hundred men and women dressed in
rags, most of them with bruised faces, too sunk to
speak, intent only to keep life in them and not be
put into the ice<i>cold ground. The huge machine of
government grinds round over their heads. That
military pomp is the toy or plaything of an autocrat.
St. Petersburg is but for those who know this con<i>
trast, and can take pleasure in it. There are sixty,
eighty, a hundred thousand, here, who live in cellars

and have not enough to eat. There is equal poverty elsewhere but not such cold. This is the prime differ-ence. Across the Baltic, in Stockholm, it was never the same, because the dregs of a nation of eighty millions did not pour into the capital and choke the cellars. This is a huge ramshackle empire, organized for wealth and loyalty, with a religion that had been sufficient in the days of simple faith, and, it could be called, a veneer of malachite or lapis lazuli that did not conceal the sordid brickwork just below. The priests with their long hair and golden robes had begun to lose their magic. A chapter to itself could be written on their golden vestments and the ritual and symbolism attached to them. They were a race apart, with hair flowing over their shoulders and beards of Assyrian cut; but in the modern slum world of over-population they had become ridicu-lous. The eternal Lazarus was turning questions in his soul. And it is known to all how he has answered them. What he destroyed was not wicked, but had outlived its day. But the circumstances are more extraordinary than in any other city in the world because of the unmeasured wealth that had accumu-lated to the Crown. It was as though the Sleeping Beauty had slept undisturbed into our times. That contradiction makes our theme; but it is more sudden and violent when we ignore its dangers. In the year we have chosen she was but turning in her sleep.

The scene becomes more and more of an hallucination. Owing to the gliding sledges and the utter silence of the snow. It is the fashionable hour. Private sledges with two or three horses harnessed abreast and liveried footmen on the step behind glide past, their Russian character apparent so this could not be New York or Montreal, then cities of the snow in winter, from the high hoop over the horses' heads, like the kokoshnik, but not hung with sleigh bells, for that is characteristic only of the Russian countryside, not of the capital, where the sleighs pass silent as a gondola. To a Western mind this scene has its direct associations with wooden houses and little towns. It is not to be expected in a city of a million souls. These are Imperial snows, not peasant scenes in a Flemish or Burgundian winter. They are Imperial, if the waters of the Bosphorus ever lost their shadows of the lattice and the caique, and are not for ever haunted. St. Petersburg can be nothing else than the ghosts of its own history. Inside those sledges there are women in crinolines, wrapped in Russian furs, sables, bearskins, and the then rare silver fox, and who, tonight, will be wearing jewels that no other Court can show. When we admit that they were born a hundred years ago, or more, from 1941, we have a vision of country houses lost, or divided from us, in an immensity of time, and now gone for ever, as though they were the empty shell of some appalling crime. These, or some of them, may be the young girls who drove past the swings and merry-go-rounds on that spring evening. Their children ride with them in the sleighs. Of whom, in some obscure corner, there could be one alive today who would remember more than other things such winter afternoons and their contrasts, made sensible today. The warmth and luxury in what, for the rich, was little else than a fairyland, and the pathos of that sense of protection which a child feels from its mother or the person it loves, and who now, in recollection, has been dead for so long a time that it was in another existence, so much has life altered. But, here, it is impossible not to enlarge upon this moment, for, after all, there must be many persons living who had like experiences for all those years, from 1868 until the last winter, when disaster came. We keep, nevertheless, to our appointed year in order to see this at a time when none doubted that it could continue.

It takes us in early spring, after the snows have melted, to estates where the peasants are still in serf- dom. Lilacs are in blossom, and nostalgia is ever present, being woven into the web or tissue of Russian life, so that misfortune would come if it were ever away for long. The landowners had large families and lived in the patriarchal way, their amount of the national temperament being proved in the number of them possessed of amateur talent. Could we, for instance, know details of the lives of many of the officers in the military review today, drawn entirely, as they were, from the landowning classes, we would find that an inordinate proportion of them were musicians, were amateur actors, or could draw or paint, but this, unexpectedly, was their weakness, and the sign that their class was doomed. Among their whole number there would be hardly a talent that could support itself. It was the proof that they had begun to doubt themselves. The legend that the Russians were artistic was the sign that their great power was slipping from their hands. No longer boyars, like their forbears, but drawing- room pianists, and everything that had been forceful

in them gone to the ineffectual and the amateur. At
the same time that the peasants lost their serfdom the
richer classes found themselves with no excuse. The
whole structure was an anomaly in the modern
world. And its surfaces were so flattering, if you did
not look beneath them into the damp cellars where
the starving lived and died.

In the Nevski Prospekt the spectacle is such as
could not be imagined by those who have not seen
it. A street three miles long and leading from the
Champs Élysées to Whitechapel or Mile End Road.
Down at the far end, which tails off as the crow
flies, towards Moscow, the buildings, the people,
and even the colour of the sky are already Asiatic,
in the extent to which that word means wars and
plagues and barbarian invasions. The first suburbs
of another and an endless world, all plains and distance. Churches and synagogues, in plenty, help
this illusion by their tawdry architecture. It could be
thus all the way from Petersburg to Peking. In the
other direction, towards the Neva, we begin to pass
great porticos and palaces. And the colonnade of
the Kazan cathedral, a semicircle of columns, barbarian echo of the Roman travertine, but which,
like the spire of the Admiralty, is in sign of St.

Petersburg. The painted shop signs, for those who cannot read, have given place to gilt lettering, dress-makers, jewellers, hairdressers. In one window the latest crinolines from Paris are displayed; or hung up in bunches like bright bird cages above the doors, all in the flaring gaslight as we glide past over the snows. Cakes and sweets in the confectioner's windows, especially at Elliseiv's, are like a child-hood's dream. We pass by a confiserie of which the sign or emblem is a little shepherd girl. The win-dows are stacked with barley sugar, in stooks and pyramids of twisted pillars, while all the fantasy of a Gallic mind, in exile, shows itself in chocolates that are shaped like marennes or portugaises of the sandy flats, ranged upon green paper, ready for sale, in the wicker baskets of the oystermen; in white hens' eggs packed in miniature wooden crates, whole and unbroken, save for an invisible perforation through which liquid chocolate has been blown in to load and fill the shells; in chocolates flecked with gold leaf; sweets in infinity flavoured with all fruits; and dragées of as many colours as there are court ladies in *The Sleeping Beauty*. The children in those sledges are children of the fashion plates of eighty years ago. Little boys in straw hats with ribbons that float out behind, with bow-ties of blue velvet, solemn black kid boots, and a long coat or paletot pulled in by a belt at the waist, like the shirt, as we have said before, of a Russian moujik: their sisters, or cousins, in long plaited pigtails, little hooped skirts ending at the knee, and little flat boatshaped hats in parody upon the fashion. More than all else, though, these are children of the goatcart. There should come that little pattering of hooves, with the sound of little wheels. A child, in rags, holds the leading rein, while the bouc, the antelope, the satyr, walks. There are two goatcarts, two goat-drawn chariots, each with a child in it, and they draw up to the Fidèle Bergère, close to that window into a world of fantasy, and pause a moment, and pass on. It is hot, very hot, and a brass band is blaring in the distance under the clipped lime trees. So might dream the shopkeeper, with head nodding upon his flowered waistcoat? Or the children, wrapped in furs, who stop while a parcel is brought out to them, and glide home over the snow?

It is to be remarked that the foreign shops have caught the spirit, or the genius loci. The Fidèle Bergère, for we do not need to hurry, we only watch the sledges gliding by, has a lavish fantasy that it

would not have in France. There is much display
of the double-headed eagle. It appears, many times
over, on the wrapping of every parcel; and there are
inventions in the window that are pure Russian. It
is thus with every Western art that has been transplanted to the Russian soil, from the cuisine à la
russe, so largely the work of Gouffet, chef-de-
cuisine to Alexander II, to the buildings of Rastrelli, Charles Cameron, Quarenghi, or Thomas de
Thomon. In fact, the Russian style, like the style à
l'espagnole, is largely a foreign creation. That is to
say, after perhaps one generation of foreign inspiration, the Russians seized upon what had been discovered for them and carried it still further. Another
sledge draws up, and a lady dressed in sables walks
into a shop, followed by a chasseur or heyduck in
gorgeous uniform. All the passers-by wear sheepskin coats down to their feet, which are wrapped
in rags. There is a multitude of beggars of the hermit
type; and persons of the Oriental slant gazing at
the lit windows. Also, innumerable grey coated
soldiers, the automatons of the crowd, for they have
but a collective personality and are not individual.
And we pass enormous private palaces, while a
street song comes from near by, and sledges at full

gallop dash round the corner of the Morskaja into the Nevski Prospekt, drawing up suddenly, for the sleigh stops of an instant, having no wheels.

Is there such a thing as Russian music, in the lesser sense of a street song, a popular music of the peasant or the crowd? It has been argued there is not. Who could be so insensitive as to deny this? The street singers are of two kinds: the kalieki and kajiteli. The first wander in the villages and from town to town, singing for their daily bread: the latter sing for their own pleasure, roysterers and boon companions, likely, also, to sing on pilgrimages and in processions of the church. The national genius comes forth from them as much as in the shape of their musical phrases as in the words they use. It is a speech or vernacular, running parallel with the spoken word and apt to have more meaning, or an import at least, that is more charged or loaded than are syllables of talk. The deepest expression of their genius is in the vocal choruses such as those that Mussorgsky employed in his operas and that were the revelation of Russian music to the Western world. Many of his songs for solo voice are of the same inspiration and could be described as in street character, for their home was at the street corner or at the door of a drinking den. Never before had this been done in music. His songs have a physical force, and a realism, which are Russian, indeed, and could be naught else. We refer, in particular, to such masterpieces as *Hopak*, *The Street Arab*, or *The Carousal*. In his operas *Boris Godounov* and *Khovantchina*, the themes which are associated with earthly power or Tsardom make known their meaning instantly and upon the moment. In a song, of course, it is not the accompaniment alone but the sound of the words that give the Russian character; an instance of which, not in realism, but in sophistication, is *After the Ball*, a song by Tchaikowsky, than which nothing could be more Russian in every turn of phrase. It lives and breathes as much in this expression of nostalgia, of fashionable disillusionment, as in folk music, or in the ostensibly and demonstrably Russian idiom of Mussorgsky.

In this year of 1868 little or nothing of such names was known. *Boris Godounov* was not yet begun. Apart from street music, the one specimen of the national style was Glinka's *Life for the Tsar*, or *Jizn sa Tsaria*, dating from 1836 and often given at the Marie Theatre. In the words of a contemporary: 'This opera affords an opportunity of studying Russian melodies and costumes.' *Life for the Tsar* was always most sumptuously mounted on the stage. This, and so far as Russian ballet was concerned, the *Koniok Gorbunok* or *The Hump-backed Horse*, the first ballet to be based on a Russian theme or fairy tale, with innocuous music by Cesare Pugni, and book by Saint-Léon who, later, wrote the libretto for *Coppélia*. *The Hump-backed Horse* was given first at the Bolshoy or Great Theatre in 1864; being followed by *Tsar Devitsa* or *The Maiden Tsar*, and *The Golden Fish*, both of these being derived, also, from national popular legends. This was all. The rest of Russian music was in embryo. As to *The Hump-backed Horse*, in the words of André Levinson: 'Three worlds confront and penetrate one another in that comical fairyland; first, the manners of the Russian moujik, his squatting dances in birch bark shoes, the samovar, the knout; then an orient in the manner of an image d'Epinal; and superimposed on these two visions, the ideal kingdom of the classic dance.' [1] It was the time of the liberation of the serfs, and false sentiment expressed itself in an aping of the masses. Romans of the decadence, in

[1] Cf. *A History of Ballet in Russia*, by C. W. Beaumont, with a preface by André Levinson, London, 1930, p. x.

the same manner, affected the dress and accents of the barbarians who would destroy them. Being foreigners, we would take the first opportunity of attending a performance of the *Koniok Gorbunok*, for it is to be preferred with Russian title, at the Bolshoy Theatre; and, not less, Glinka's *Life for the Tsar* at the Marie Theatre. In 1868 we are still among the primitives of Russian music. The only other name is that of Dargomyjsky. His opera *Russalka* was already written, and he is to be remembered, too, for his *Finnish Fantasy*, with its curiously different treatment of a theme which was, afterwards, to become the drunken song of the monk Varlam in *Boris Godounov*; and for a Kosachok or Cossack dance. But Russian music, till now, is only in reality Glinka and no one else.

It could be said with truth that the first and last piece of Russian music ever written was Glinka's *Kamarinskaya*, a symphonic treatment of two Russian airs, a wedding song and dance song. This was written in 1848. Let *Kamarinskaya* speak for itself! The first simple utterance of that Russian theme is not a tune, only, but a landscape and a people. It has no date. The material is all the mediaeval centuries, in the sense in which that miracle could be achieved in a line of poetry, with this difference that Glinka did not write the tune, he discovered it and gave it immortality. In its origin it can have been no better than a hundred other Russian airs, but his genius sharpened and pointed it, so that it is, at once, Rus⁄ sian and individual, of Glinka's own. The dance song that follows it, so Russian and characteristic in its preluding, in the manner in which announce⁄ ment is made that it is coming, points the alternative season of the year. The first tune is the Russian winter: this is a long summer night, miles from anywhere, lost in the huge distances, among the wooden houses of a remote village, in a haze of dust while the immense sun is setting. Nothing of an outer world has come to them. All has been the same for centuries, since the time that they were pagan. The false notes of the last strophe are an in⁄ spiration, and the birth of a new school of music. Never before had this been attempted. The school of discord has its authority from this.

But Glinka made other discoveries no less im⁄ portant. He went to Madrid, a journey without pre⁄ cedent for a Russian of the reign of Nicholas I, and had the intention to compose a Spanish opera. He lodged overlooking the Puerta del Sol, and took

down the melodies of flamenco singers and guitar-
ists, including seguidillas manchegas from a mule-
teer. Later, he visited Granada. The results of his
Spanish journey were the *Jota Aragonesa* and *Summer
Night in Madrid*. Most unfortunately, he never per-
severed in a proposed work to be based upon Anda-
lucian melodies, which would have been a study of
the flamenco style. But these are, at least, the first
serious orchestral works in Spanish idiom. Glinka's
other compositions are the delightful Valse-Fan-
taisie, a picture of the salons or ballrooms of St.
Petersburg; and, for historical importance, such
pieces as the krakoviak and mazurka from *Life for
the Tsar*, together with the lezghinka and other
dances from *Ruslan and Liudmila*. It must be said of
these two operas that the first, in spite of certain
moments or set numbers, is still written in a hybrid
style, with touches of Weber, or even Nicolai. But
the lezghinka, described by Glinka himself, as a
'Grand Air de danse sur des thèmes du Caucase et
de la Crimèe', and composed for double orchestra,
is the first contact of a Russian composer with the
Orient of Caucasus and Caspian. *Ruslan* has, as
well, a Persian chorus and melodies of Tartar origin.
Beyond these experiments lie the magic lands of

Central Asia, leading to Samarcand and to Bok-
hara. Glinka, indeed, not only composed the first
Russian opera and the first Russian songs, but he
discovered the national style of music in *Kamarinskaya*, while he made the earliest experiments in
Spanish music and in music of the Orient. And he
was an amateur and philanderer, lazy as only Russians with aesthetic tastes can be; and it is interesting to note for such details have their psycho-
logical importance, no more than 5 ft. $\frac{3}{8}$ inches
tall, nearly related, in fact, to the dwarf, being less
than two inches removed from that defined frontier.
Repin, in his well-known portrait of Glinka, lying
on a sofa in a flowered dressing gown, his music
table at his elbow, gives him the strong and aquiline
features which must be the cause and explanation of
his contradictory character. His small stature is not
apparent in the picture. Perhaps it is, even, pur-
posely concealed. But the features are those of a remarkable and determined man, typically enough,
for the most Russian of all composers is concerned,
not at all Slav or Russian in appearance. For the
first half of the nineteenth century in Russia the most
important figures are the Tsar himself (Nicholas I),
Pushkin, and Glinka. During the second half of

the century they will be Tolstoy, Dostoievsky, and Mussorgsky. These later names are a clear indication of the trend towards revolution. But our chosen moment of 1868, which is a visual impression, takes note only of the present and the immediate past. The future is not within its province. We can only discuss Russian music in so far as it had been achieved by then. For opera and ballet we have to be content with Glinka and *The Humpbacked Horse*.

That side of the Russian dilettante which delighted in *Koniok Gorbunok* or in *Life for the Tsar* was already beginning to discover Moscow. For a hundred and fifty years, since the founding of St. Petersburg, the old capital had been altogether neglected in favour of the new. Moscow was left to the merchants and the provincials. It was a mistaken historical sense that made Napoleon attack the heart of Russia in the 1812 campaign. Had he gone, instead, to St. Petersburg the Grande Armée could have maintained itself through the winter and completed its conquests with the melting of the snows. But it was the old focus and centre of the nation that destroyed him. It was here that the racial character was preserved, unspoilt by the straight streets and classical façades of the West. To the devout Russian, Moscow was the Third Rome, to which the Church and the true religion were transferred after the fall of Byzantium. St. Petersburg, the artificial creation of one man, could never compete in this. Moscow was Russia: St. Petersburg, the bastard child of Russian adultery with the manners and fashions of the West. For the history of the future it is a curious detail to find how few Russians of St. Petersburg, that is to say of the wealthy or intellectual classes, had even seen the old capital, and what an effect, with their reviving nationalism, it had upon them. In illustration, Mussorgsky first visited Moscow in 1859, having been encouraged to do so by Balakirev, who had been there the year before. Balakirev had written to him—and part of the charm of the Russian school of composers is the prompt naïveté with which they communicated their opinions to each other—that, in the Kremlin: 'he had felt with pride that he was Russian'. To this, Mussorgsky replied, a year later: 'I have been a cosmopolitan, but now I have undergone a sort of re-birth; I have been brought nearer to everything Russian . . . St. Basil's worked on me so pleasantly and yet so strangely that it seemed as if at any moment a boyar might appear in long smock and high cap'. He was thrilled by the Red Square, the Spassky Gate, the Cathedral of the Archangels, and the bell-tower of Ivan the Great. 'Moscow has taken me into another world, the world of antiquity, a dirty world . . . the earth has never produced such rogues and beggars.' In these phrases the future composer of *Boris Godounov* is speaking.

The coronation of the Tsars took place in Moscow and was occasion for the most extraordinary display of pageantry. More particularly during the nineteenth century, upon the three occasions of Alexander II in 1856, Alexander III in 1881, and Nicholas II in 1894. The most magnificent of all was that of Alexander II in 1856, at a time before criticism upon such expenditure had become general. The details of this wonderful display are to be studied in a volume of such immense size that the term 'elephant folio' has no meaning, and, indeed, this may be the largest book that has ever issued from the printing press. It requires two men to carry it, even in the North Library of the British Museum. Moreover, and this has another interest, it is printed throughout, or in fact, lithographed, in golden letters, in an archaic, or Byzantine style, of which this is, probably, the earliest instance in Russia. The text is in French; and there are huge coloured lithographs, and more curious still, drawings which must have been made upon the spot and that are reproduced, in woodcut, in the text. Not works of art, but fascinating in their improbability.

From this work, and other sources, including a volume of letters from Comte Achille Murat, attached to the delegation from Napoleon III, we learn that the first sign of the impending celebrations could have been noticed on a late afternoon in St. Petersburg, when a large detachment of the Chevaliers Gardes in their eagle helmets, white uniforms and silver breastplates, were seen riding slowly, sword in hand, at a walking pace, surrounding certain locked and closed waggons, down the far end of the Nevski Prospekt, in the direction of the Moscow railway station.

At this point in that long street the magnificence of St. Petersburg has been left behind. It is the region of shabby shops, painted red and yellow, and vodka cellars where, at all hours of the day or night, there are peasants singing drunken songs. A district of endless open spaces, with the peculiar poetry of

waste and emptiness. Wooden palings that hold
nothing back, garbage heaps, terrible hovels, and
always music, as though it were a drug or intoxicant
in this misery. Different from the Gypsy music of
the restaurants upon the islands? Ah! not so different; and, perhaps, more certain in its purpose.
For that is hired with money. Here, it is themselves
for whom they play. This land of broken stones and
sherds is a world to itself, ending in the swamps and
marshes. In the proximity of the railway station it
becomes romantic with the steam whistle and the
shunting of trucks. But, in all, it is an endless pro-
spect of misery and poverty. The spectacle, in midst
of this, of the Chevaliers Gardes was as unusual as
that of the Life Guards in a London slum. Not less
so, because this long street ends, in appearances, in
Asia. It leads from marble palaces and granite quays
to the suburbs of Peking. Above, the winter sun
throws its light on silver breastplates in the desert
space opposite the station.

It is the escort taking the Crown and jewels of
Russia to be entrained for Moscow. At previous
coronations they have gone the whole way by road,
and three weeks have been spent upon the journey.
The Imperial Crown of all the Russias, hidden,

like a totem or a fetich, is carried past the pawn shops and the vodka dens, wrapped up like an idol and enclosed in many boxes. Could our eyes pierce the wooden packing cases, and the sealed vehicle which is like an ammunition waggon, this is the Imperial Crown. It is shaped like the mitre of a patriarch. The summit is a cross formed of five diamonds, held up by an uncut but polished spinel ruby. An arch of eleven great diamonds, springing from back to front, supports this ruby and its cross, and there is a side arch or hoop of pearls. This gives the mitre shape; while the rim or band is a row of twenty-eight huge diamonds. The crown of the Tsarina is nothing else but diamonds, but more feminine and more typically Russian in design. There are other wonders of the diamond world: double and triple necklaces of diamonds: pearls worthy of the Ptolemies: and the collar, star, and jewel of the Order of St. Andrew, of pink diamonds, and beryls or aquamarines of Siberia, worn by the Tsar only for his coronation. Also, the Orb of all the Russias, topped by a diamond of the finest water and by a greenish sapphire. By the side of the waggons march Court servants in their liveries, and the front and rear are closed by troops.

The other waggons, for there are ten or twelve of them, must contain robes and insignia and uniforms of gala. The gilded coaches have already left for Moscow, some of them weeks ago, by road, mounted on huge drays. But this departure of the Crown and jewels is the first signal. Next day, and the days following, many persons leave for Moscow by the afternoon train. Soon, the fashionable quarters of the capital are deserted. The guests, for there are few hotels in Moscow, are lodged in private houses, and in wooden palaces put up for the occasion. Meanwhile, the coaches and baggage waggons are arriving. And the Tsar and Royal family reach Moscow on the eve, and stay, according to custom, at the Petrovsky palace in the suburbs, built by Paul I, a sham Gothic red pavilion, ramshackle, half-furnished, in every sense temporary, but of immense size, with a whole town of temporary wooden structures set up round it for the occasion.

Next morning, after long hours of waiting, the procession comes through the Spasköi Vorota, or Gate of the Redeemer, into the vast open square of the Kremlin. In front is the Uspenski Sobor, the Cathedral of the Assumption. All round, in every direction, there are domes and spires. The gilded crosses on the churches rise from crescents. There are domes like melons, pumpkins, pineapples, like pears or strawberries, painted in all colours, orna‑ mented with disks and stars, and hung with veils of gilded chains. The procession is more than a mile in length, and does not come forward in a straight line but curves and zigzags in perfect order, and as though to be the better seen. Squadrons of the Che‑ valiers Gardes and Gardes à cheval come first, in their gilded or their silver breastplates. After various dignitaries, growing in importance, the state car‑ riages begin and, at last, the gilded coaches. The extraordinary and unique feature in this procession is the manner in which the Imperial insignia are exhibited in open carriages or chariots, no bigger than a sledge and holding two persons, sitting side by side. The steps of these gilded chariots are en‑ crusted with real diamonds, emeralds, and rubies— or false stones—it does not matter which, but their effect is that of a magical circus entrance, enhanced by the plumes and panaches of the horses and of the coachmen or postillions. Horses of a light breed, not the black and heavy Russian Orlovs, draw these gilded cars. In the first, ride the two Masters of Cere‑

monies, heralds or precursors of this magic moment. The splendour and fantasy of these light equipages, dating mostly from the reign of the Tsarina Elizabeth, is the more effective against this background of the Tartar Rome. That world of cornucopia or gilded seashell from which these gay chariots and their occupants derive, which is that of the masque and poetry of the Western Renaissance but come down in scale to the gilded pleasure barge or golden sledge, has travelled far abroad. The cars of Neptune have become the toy or plaything of the Russian boyar; and to our taste this procession is more farfetched and fanciful than the Carrousels of Le Roi Soleil. A gilded phaeton follows in which the Court Marshal Prince Michel Kotchoubey displays a baton, topped or ornamented with a huge emerald. In another light phaeton, open, or in the official term *découvert*, upholstered in crimson velvet, come two Masters of Ceremonies holding in their right hands long silver bâtons surmounted by a golden double-headed eagle. Behind them, Count Borch, Grand Master of Ceremonies, with his golden baton ornamented with a great emerald. Immediately behind him, two dignitaries with numbers after their names, as though from a ballet programme, carry in one hand their gilded wands of office, and we see their gilt shoes, and satin breeches and white stockings. When the chariot draws up, they will alight with a dancing step and wait for the golden coach in which the Tsarina rides. But it is not in sight. All these precursors have their distinc⁄ tive and symbolic costumes. They are followed by a solid body of Court servants, headed by the major domos, and ending with eighty valets in their liveries of gala.

Next come twenty⁄four huntsmen in red and green liveries, from the kennels at Gatchina, and the Master of the Hounds, the Grand Veneur, Prince Dimitri Wassiltschikev. We have to see him, in imagination, by the lake upon an autumn afternoon, cast for the role of Benno, the Prince's friend, in *Le Lac des Cygnes*. There is a mist above the water, and lovely swans float down from the sky and settle near the reeds. We catch familiar but distant music, that nostalgic open melody of Tchaikowsky, and far off through the trees an enchanted castle, but no more improbable than the truth of Gatchina or Tsarskoe Selo. And the music dies away. Other figures come into the mind. More lacqueys or valets: the Tsar's boatmen. The choristers of the Imperial chapel, brought from St. Petersburg, dressed in scarlet cloaks. More Court servants in the mottled red and brown liveries of the Imperial household. Other dignitaries and Court officials. A number of Court carriages, some with four, and some with six horses; postillions in English style, in blue and silver jackets and velvet jockey caps, or monteros, of Charles II style, descended from the Spanish muleteers, with powdered wigs; coachmen in scarlet great coats with capes. The horses that draw these carriages are the black Orlovs. Their burden is more heavy. The *jeunes premiers*, in their light chariots, have gone in front. The wheels of the great coaches, with their gilt spokes, creak and rumble on the sanded square.

In early times the point of such processions was to display the Tsar's household, and while his retinue comes closer and closer to his sacred person, we could almost expect to see the chefs and scullions, the wine tasters, and the silver wine cisterns, even the mute orchestra of the batterie de cuisine. Instead, a higher strain of fantasy is reached. Six of the skorok- hods or Court runners come past in their peculiar dress, and following them, eight huge negroes *en grand panache*. No more need be said of either skorokhods or Court Arabs, for the moment, since they are Palace servants and will be on duty at the ball tonight. The biggest and most golden of the coaches, surmounted by an Imperial crown, drawn by eight bay horses caparisoned with golden harness and housings of garnet-coloured velvet, holds the Dowager Empress, Alexandra Feodorowna. The interior of her coach is upholstered with the same garnet velvet; and the coachmen and piqueurs walking by its side wear liveries of the same colour and material. Two little pages in plumed hats sit on the box, with their backs to the coachmen and look-ing into the coach. The horses' heads are decorated with white ostrich plumes and glands de stras, or tassels made of paste and glittering like diamonds. Behind, come two palefreniers à cheval, and four Cossacks of the Household. Next, and in the same state of Cossacks and palefreniers with walking footmen at the side, comes the Tsarina in a coach drawn by eight gray horses with harness and hous-ings of silver and blue velvet. The interior of this coach of the Tsarina Maria Alexandrovna is up-holstered in 'ponceau' velvet. Riding behind them are a body of one hundred nobles and gentlemen in the ancient boyar dress, who precede the Tsar. He wears a general's uniform with the blue ribbon and

star of the Order of St. Andrew. The Mamelukes
of the Guard come close behind him, then the
Cossacks, and the Horse Guards, and coach after
coach filled with the Grand Dukes and their
families, in strict precedence: the Red Hussars, the
Preobrajenski, the Pavlovski, the Tirailleurs de la
Garde: more and more regiments: more bands of
martial music.

At the door of the Uspenski Sobor the archbishop
and metropolitans are waiting. The five domes of
the cathedral, in symbol of the metropolitan and his
five deacons, have been repainted with leaf gold for
this occasion, and the whole hierarchy, in heaven
and upon earth, contrasts with the temporal or
secular world. Their vestments and the bulbous
shapes of the Byzantine mitre, their long beards, and
the purple or golden klobouk, a high cap with a
veil covering it and falling on the shoulders, are of
this Orient of the snows, a winter lasting for a thousand years, in which the Eastern complexity and
extravagance have found a refuge.

This is the priesthood of the Tartar Rome. They
hold in their hands sacred icons, the relics of saints,
and the shepherd's crook burgeoning into a hundred
floreated shapes, until it has become a staff, a thur-

ible, a sacred thyrsus. The Tsar with his own hand
will place the crown upon his head, standing in the
ivory throne which Sophia Palaeologus brought
with her to Russia.[1] He will be wearing the por-
phyri, a purple robe or coat, worn only upon this
day and stored, afterwards, in the Orujeinaya Pa-
lata, or treasury; and, over it, the Imperial mantle
made of gold glazeta, with double-headed eagles
sewn upon it, lined with pure white ermine on
which are scattered numerous jet black tails. The
gilded and painted interior of the Uspenski Sobor
is shown filled with the great men of the Empire
and their wives, and the delegates of every foreign
country. On another page we see the coronation
banquet, with silver plate from the treasury in
Moscow, or brought from St. Petersburg, stacked
on the tables and ranged in great buffets nearly to
the ceiling. The Grand Ecuyer hands the golden
dishes to the Tsar, walking the whole length of the
banqueting hall escorted by two officers of the

[1] Upon her marriage with Ivan III in 1472. It is not probable that Sophia Palaeologus brought the ivory throne from
Constantinople, since the Turks took that city in 1453. The
history of the throne is, therefore, uncertain; but, at least, her
marriage confirmed the Byzantine ritual and ceremonial in
Russia.

Chevaliers Gardes with drawn swords. The Grand Échanson hands the Tsar a golden cup to drink from. The banquet lasts for several hours. And, in the last plate in this book we are given, for contrast, the popular rejoicings. Swings and merry-go-rounds and montagnes russes. A crowd of tens of thousands, of whom in a panic many hundreds may be trampled underfoot. The young moujiks with their hair cropped for the Coronation and an air, therefore, of varlets or knaves from the playing cards; and their fathers, who may have fought against Napoleon, serfs not yet liberated but belonging to their masters, and classed as so many hundred souls to give them a difference from herds of cattle. It is even drawn in popular or moujik style, if anything, accenting the broad faces and low fringes of the peasants. Moreover, most of them are depicted as already drunk, as though there was no doubt of this and it was expected of them. It was the tradition, just as the Celestial smokes his pipe of opium. And we close the back cover of this giant book with the grinding of steam organs, the singing of choruses, and rhythms of hopak and trepak, still ringing in our ears.

Afternoon has faded into evening. In this strange

city of St. Petersburg it is much more alive. For that twilight was as another dawn. The last regiments at the review had marched off an empty square into a mistless but grey emptiness. Out of sight their military music had struck up again, which the wind carried in blasts and snatches down the granite streets. In every direction, from all over the town. Along the frozen Neva. Off that sheet of ice. Through the air, heavy with snowflakes falling with deadening sound. Their barracks must be grey poor-houses or infirmaries, with food of grey gruel or skilly, and greying bread. But the brass music comes again. The lights burn up in all the town. In an instant the snow becomes a carpet or soft covering laid down, in winter, because it is beautiful and white. Every roof and surface has its snowy outline, which is like the heightening with gold or silver in a drawing. The shapes and colours of the military uniforms, and anticipation of the ball to-night, invoke, for a moment or two, the domes and spires of Moscow, while the night darkens. For it is, now, a winter evening. The whole of snowy Asia, by way of Moscow, ends in this city, that looks out on to a frozen sea. Lit with gas, not electricity. A yellowish or reddish glare, with long lines of lights down by the Neva, continuing, in a haze, on to the islands. The lights of the Nevski Prospekt, as it might be, a long canal running through the centre of the town. And the whole city transformed, or made transcendental, in the snow, not only from that crystal whiteness, but in the noiseless gliding of the sledges, and from the silent footfalls all along the street.

It is time to go home and rest a little. How will other persons have passed their day? In order to con-trast the cold and misery, that are working for re-venge, with this luxury beyond parallel, it is more pointed not to mention them. Let us, therefore, examine this luxury from first-hand evidence. In his book of memoirs, General Mossolov gives a detailed picture that must be augmented in its scale and colouring for every decade that recedes into the past. He writes of the Court of Nicholas II, though with personal memories of the reign of Alexander III and even before that.[1] His account must, therefore, be magnified when it is transferred from 1910 to 1868.

[1] *At the Court of the last Tsar*, by A. A. Mossolov, edited by A. A. Pilenko, Methuen & Co., London, 1935. This is by far the most detailed book of memories of the Russian Court.

Of the world outside the windows nothing need be said. The aftermath is too well known. This is the palace of the Caesars in its last travesty, beginning with the Golden House of Nero, and come down from Byzantium. Influenced, also, by Le Roi Soleil, and created in fresh travesty of splendour by Cathe/ rine the Great and her grandson, Nicholas I; sur/ viving, indeed, into the lifetime of most persons who will read these lines. In order to apprehend its especial character it is better to quote from this book of faded glories, where the author remarks: 'The principal function of a sovereign's Court is to in/ crease his prestige', continuing: 'The Russian Court was certainly the most opulent in Europe. Great wealth had been accumulating during three hundred years in the hands of those responsible for its safe keeping.' Certain Moscovite customs and manner/ isms had become mingled, by tradition, into this magnificence. At the back of it, again, or under/ neath, all was essentially Russian. The surface was Western, as though in copy of Versailles; but it was barbarian in scale and execution, while its final spangling, the ultimate gold or silver pencilling of its edges, once more was characteristically Russian. This is true of everything that has to do with the

Petersburg period, as it is called. We noticed it, even in the shops along the Nevski Prospekt. In the shop window of the Fidèle Bergère; on a Russian menu; in the architecture of Cameron or Rastrelli; in the music of Tchaikowsky's ballets. These, for instance, are based deliberately upon Delibes, but how different in the result! Delibes, for all his talent, and because of the nature of that, was not capable of those long open airs, those romantic interludes. They are in the Italian manner, strongly influenced by Mozart and by Bellini; but could they be mistaken for anything but Russian! They are entire, of that nation, in their accent and their intonation. Nothing but Russian in their meaning and their symbolism. The Russian atmosphere was as strong, also, in its effect upon artists of foreign blood. There is as much evidence of this truth as there are proofs that, in Spain, the native genius had to be formed and stimulated from outside. Until this was done, they were not certain of their own direction. And so it was in Russia, beginning with the buildings of the Kremlin.[1] It is one of the mysteries of architecture

---

[1] The Spasköi Vorota, or Gate of the Redeemer, was built by the Milanese architect, Pietro Solario, in 1491, and other towers of the Kremlin by Antonio Aleviso. The Ca-

that such complicated disorder, appearing to be the work of many centuries, should have been accom‧plished in a single generation. They are as inchoate and anonymous as the Romanesque or Gothic. This Tartar *coup d'œil* was the invention, in the first place, of Italians; and, in lesser degree, of Germans and Flemings. But it is entirely Russian, more Rus‧sian, as to the Cathedral of St. Basil and the Krem‧lin, than anything else in Russia. Catherine the Great, a German, was as much of a Russian as Peter the Great. Such contradictions are typical of Russia.

The Winter Palace, with its half‧mile of great apartments on three floors, along the Neva, could have been built in no city but St. Petersburg. Even the fact that nearly the whole of its interior was des‧troyed by fire in 1837, and rebuilt within a year, has made little difference to the original intention. In‧ternally, it is largely a series of great halls, of no particular importance in themselves, decorated

thedral of the Assumption, or Uspenski Sobor, was the work of Aristotele Fioraventi of Bologna, who had been in the employment of Cosimo de' Medici, Gian Galeazzo Sforza, François I, and Sixtus IV. Even the Cathedral of St. Basil, most extreme yet typical of Russian buildings, is as‧cribed to an Italian.

chiefly in the style of Nicholas I, and forming a suit-
able background for the pomp of Court ceremonies.
At the same time, and owing to the scale of these,
it is more interesting than the generality of Royal
palaces in their ugliness and monotony. It com-
pares, in ordinary, with the palaces of Caserta and
Madrid. But the Russian extravagance puts it by
itself; while as a residence for the Russian Court, it
has to be considered in relation to Tsarskoe Selo and
Gatchina, and to the other summer palaces, big or
little, to which its fantastic inhabitants were dis-
persed from the capital. The anomaly of such exist-
ences makes our subject; but, also, the routine of
their lives. It seems not to have occurred to them
that their doom was sealed. They were fortified, or
we may think, hypnotized, by the splendour of their
surroundings. So far as personal authority was concerned, this was the greatest Empire in the world,
an absolute autocracy, justified by its extraordinary
successes in the past. The individuals composing
the Court lived in an enchanted world, an organic
body, if those persons are discussed who lived in
the various palaces, which had been flourishing,
at least, since the reign of the Tsarina Elizabeth
Petrovna (1741–1761), and like all bodies thriving on

so rich a soil, has developed into peculiar forms, and a profuse or excessive blossoming. Little by little it increased its character, imperceptibly, and repre-senting that each further growth was inevitable, so that the Tsars, themselves, were unwilling to cur-tail them. It is in this way that the Court survived, and even augmented itself, during the reign of Nicholas I, with all his passion for utility and detail. Under Alexander II, while the mineral wealth of the imperial properties came pouring in, there was no reason for economy. The Empire was spreading through Central Asia[1] and was, by repute, the great military power of Europe; master of Asia, and perpetual menace to the Indies. In these circum-stances an extravagant Court was an outward sign of power. It further increased, therefore, in impro-bability, reaching its climax about the time at which we see it. After the murder of Alexander II, his successor, who had simpler tastes and cared little for ceremony, did nothing to encourage its further growth, though both under himself and his suc-cessor Nicholas II it flourished unchecked. But the great ceremonies were abandoned, somewhat, after

[1] Tashkent was occupied by Russia in 1865: Samarcand in 1868: Khiva in 1873.

1903. The unfortunate course taken by the Russo-
Japanese war, followed by the abortive revolution of
1905, together with the last Tsarina's love of retire-
ment, and hatred of being seen in public, combined
together so that the organization remained in being
but functioned no more. So it continued, until the
war and the revolution. Splendours necessitated by
the state of the Empress Catherine, or of Nicholas I,
and which were outward and visible proof of their
historical importance, survived through two more
generations and were only extinguished in the holo-
caust.

If we were living in the palace the morning would
begin, not too early, with a breakfast of three kinds
of bread. This was no different, till lately, in the
modern luxury hotel.[1] But it was followed by the
'kalatch', a roll of white bread, brought in a warm
napkin and eaten hot, made with water brought
specially from the river Moskva. It was the peculiar
bread of Moscow; [2] and this Moskva water was sent

[1] A contemporary authority ascribes to Catherine the
Great the first employment of plate glass windows. The
luxury of one generation becomes the commonplace, and
then the bugbear, of the next.

[2] 'Kalatches, a species of roll with what looks as if intended for a handle. The last mentioned bread is peculiar to

to the palaces near St. Petersburg, and even to the Crimea when the Court was there. General Mossolov describes the kalatch, and the still more curious ceremony of the *présent*. This dated from the eighteenth century. It will be agreed that, in imagery, it is so Russian as scarcely to be believed. This could only take place at the Court of King Florestan, while the Sleeping Beauty lay sleeping. It was a law or decree, which had begun as a spontaneous offering, by which the Ural Cossacks brought to the Tsar, every spring, the first haul of their year's fishing. Holes were cut in the ice, nets were lowered, and while the priests sprinkled incense, the fish and the caviar were packed in waggons and sent direct to St. Petersburg, with a Cossack deputation. On arrival, the sturgeon and the three sorts of caviar were carried into the great dining room of the Winter Palace. The Tsar received the Cossacks, and they were rewarded. After this the *présent* went the round of the Grand Dukes and Court officials. Count Mossolov as Head of the Court Chancellery being given five or six fine sturgeons, a yard

Moscow, where there are upwards of ninety establishments that bake nothing else.' Quoted from *A Journey to St. Petersburg and Moscow through Courland and Livonia*, by Leitch Ritchie, London, 1836, p. 209.

long, and some forty pounds of caviar for his share.

Who were the Court officials? Count Mossolov gives the following figures, for the year 1908. Fifteen of the first class, with titles of Grand Chamberlain, Grand Marshal, Master of the Imperial Hunt and Grand Cup Bearer. Belonging to the second class, 134 officials who rendered actual services, and 86 given honorary positions: the two Grand Masters of Ceremonies, the Grand Écuyer trenchant, the Huntsmen, the Marshals, the Director of the Imperial Theatres, the Director of the Hermitage Museum, and the Masters of Ceremonies (14 active and 14 honorary). There were, as well, 287 Chamberlains, 309 Gentlemen-in-Waiting, 110 persons attached to the Imperial Family; 22 priests, 38 doctors, 3 harbingers (whoever harbingers may be!), 18 valets and 150 officers. Adding to these 240 ladies in waiting, of various degrees, attached to the Imperial Court and the different Grand Ducal Courts, and 66 ladies belonging to the Order of St. Catherine, the total reached is 1,543 persons in all. And this is, of course, exclusive of all Court servants.

To this list of the Court of King Florestan XXIV we would add Cantalbutte, Master of the Cere-

monies; Ministers of State; the Fairy of the Pine
Woods and her Page; the Cherry Blossom Fairy;
the Fairy of the Humming Birds: of the Song Birds:
of the Mountain Ash; the Lilac Fairy; the Carna-
tion Fairy; all with their pages or train bearers; the
Witch Carabosse; Royal Nurses; Royal Pages; the
King's Herald; the Royal Physician; the Spanish
Prince; the Indian Prince; the Italian Prince; the
English Prince (probably, indeed, the Prince of
Wales, afterwards Edward VII, King-Emperor,
for he was married to the Tsarina's sister); Prince
Charming and the Princess Aurora and her friends,
skilled in the *adagio*; Ladies-in-Waiting, Lords,
Pages, Court Negroes, village youths and maidens,
Gardeners, Duchesses, Dukes, Baronesses, Marchio-
nesses, Marquises, Huntsmen, Nymphs, Beaters,
Servants and dignitaries of the Court. In fact, the
princed programme of *The Sleeping Beauty*.

Two parallel worlds were in being, the true and
the false. This latter derived from the Imperial
School of Dancing, which produced the most
famous dancers of the modern world. It was Paul I
who established the Imperial School, for both sexes,
in a palace between the Nevski Prospekt and the
Fontanka Canal, and engaged Didelot, the great

choreograph, to teach the pupils. From 1801 until
1917 the Imperial School trained dancers for the
Maryinsky Theatre. The regime was austere or military. The girl pupils were dressed as though at a
convent school; the boys are described, in the life
of Nijinsky,[1] as receiving three uniforms; black for
everyday, dark blue for the holidays, grey linen for
the summer; a silver lyre was embroidered on their
velvet collars; they were allowed two overcoats, one
with a collar of astrachan; and patent-leather boots.
Eventually, after eight years of tuition, they would
graduate to the Maryinsky Theatre and disappear
into its corps de ballet of a hundred and eighty
dancers. In addition to their special training they
were given a good education. They visited the
museums; they walked in a crocodile along the
Nevski Prospekt, after breakfast, and of course
wearing their patent-leather boots and their military
caps with the double-headed eagle, in gold, upon
the front; in the evening they were driven to the
theatre, boys and girls apart, in landaus from the
Imperial Stables.

Upon occasion, in those same landaus, they were

[1] *Nijinsky*, by Romola Nijinsky, Victor Gollancz, London, 1933.

taken to the theatre in the Hermitage, where they performed before the Tsar and his family. This little theatre is a building by Quarenghi. It is not large and has no boxes. The stalls rise in the form of an amphitheatre, as in Palladio's theatre at Vicenza, and in front are armchairs for the Imperial Family. This theatre, which was added in 1780, connects with the rest of the Hermitage by a bridge thrown over a canal, the arch, itself, being occupied by a foyer or anteroom, lit on each side by lofty windows, and giving views over the Neva and the street of the Milionaya. The façade of this theatre, with its pilas-tered front and recesses filled with statues, is a masterpiece of Quarenghi and, after his portico to the manège of the Gardes à cheval, his best building in St. Petersburg. As to the Maryinsky Theatre, that was designed by Rossi, last of the classical architects in Russia. It was here that the dancers of the Imperial Ballet gave their performances. The whole of the expenses both of the school and the theatre were borne by the Tsar's privy purse, and under Nicholas II, after the public had paid for their seats there was often an annual deficit of two hundred thousand pounds to be met. Such was the price paid by an autocrat for the art of Russian

dancing. To the income of the Tsars it was equivalent to no more than the upkeep of a yacht.

This income, which was estimated in 1914 at
twelve million pounds a year, was raised from house
property in the capital, and from immense tracts of
forest. Also, from the mines of Nertchinsk and
Altai, where there were gold and precious stones.
This was apart from the civil list which paid the
expenses of the Court. The Grand Dukes of the
Romanov family were supported by the apanages,
apart again from any private fortunes they may have
possessed. The apanages were a fund started by
Paul I (who, in spite of his madness, left a mark
after a reign of only five years) in order to place the
Imperial family upon an independent basis. It was
derived from real estate, and was calculated so as
to allow each Grand Duke and Grand Duchess,
from birth, an income of twenty-eight thousand
pounds. When it is considered that, during the nineteenth century, there was an average of thirty males
and rather more females in the Romanov family,
this is a formidable sum. And yet, according to
General Mossolov, the apanages had been so care-
fully managed that, in 1914, there was a liquid
reserve amounting to six million pounds. The third

generation, great grandsons and daughters of a Tsar, had the right only to a single payment of a hundred thousand pounds. This good fortune was rather mitigated by Alexander III, who decreed that in future only sons and grandsons of a Tsar shared benefit from the apanages. Until his time, any member of the family married in the knowledge that all his children would receive, at birth, that princely income. The proverbial extravagance of the Russian Grand Dukes had this excuse for it. That they should spend their money in Paris or on the Riviera had become the tradition; and, after Nicholas I, little was done to educate them to any other view of life.

In the knowledge of a few details of this wild economy, for it had its system and was managed with prudence so that it paid its way, a picture of this beautiful city rises up, once more, before our eyes. We see the orange-painted Roumianzov palace on the Granite Quay, with its tremendous colonnade, a coloured architecture so different from the grey Palladian of England. The Ministry of Justice, painted blue, another classical building of which the effect would be most striking, whether in the golden summer, or in the powdery blue snow.

## THE PAVLOVSKI GUARDS

Yellow is the colour of the Pavlovski Barracks, a long low flight of building of a bastard Greek, dwarfed like the colonnades of Paestum among the asphodels, and destined in St. Petersburg for that snub-nosed regiment of Paul I who wore the copper mitre of the Prussian Grenadier. That facial qualification for admission to the regiment was faithfully adhered to. It is even said that Nicholas I caught the chill which caused his death when choosing recruits for enrolment in the Pavlovski during the Crimean War.

There are many of the painted façades in St. Petersburg; but from contemporary evidence the manège of the Gardes à cheval was most admired of all. It was painted green, having a portico of eight Doric columns of white granite, and a good sculptured pediment of athletes taming horses. The architect is Quarenghi, and the date 1804. After St. Isaac's Cathedral and the Hermitage, it was the different manèges or Riding Schools of the Guards regiments that formed the main interest of the capital. More than the palaces or churches; and proving, in this, the predominant military aspect of St. Petersburg, a city of uniforms inhabited, at times, by as many as eighty thousand of the Imperial Guard.

Everyone knew, at sight, the black horses of the
Gardes à cheval: the chestnuts of the Chevaliers
Gardes: the dapple greys of the Gatchina Hussars:
the Mamelukes of the Guard, as they were called,
escorting the Emperor, and divided into Lezghines
in pointed helms and coats of mail, like warriors of
the Crusades, and Tcherkesses armed with carbines,
but carrying, as well, a bow and arrows in a quiver
slung across their backs. There were always Cossacks, in quantity, riding in the streets; of the Imperial Guard, in scarlet kosakhins, with long close
fitting coats and gilt bandoliers; Ataman Cossacks
in their uniforms of sapphire blue; and Cossacks of
the Black Sea in crimson coats, of whom the
officers wore a curious round cap of Persian or
Caucasian influence, gold braided, and with a
little quilted peak, more like a woman's cap worn
in the harem. If they were extremely tall, and thin,
the appearance was peculiar, being taken from the
dress of the adolescents in the tribes towards the
Caucasus. All of these regiments had their manège
or riding school where the troops could exercise
when there was snow outside. Not that the most
severe degree of cold was ever allowed to interfere
with the Imperial parades. It was the custom of

Nicholas I to arrive on the parade ground in a plain
sledge, out of which he stepped with no coat over
his uniform, and often without gloves. In the great
parades it often happened that many of the soldiers
were badly frostbitten; and it requires no imagination to picture the sufferings of the raw recruits.

These painted façades, coloured like the coats of
soldiers, may have been the invention of Rastrelli
in the reign of the Empress Elizabeth, but they continued till the time of Nicholas I. It was a Russian
custom, first applied by Rastrelli to buildings in the
Italian manner. Quarenghi, whose name must
occur so often in any account of St. Petersburg,
came from Bergamo, and is the equal and contemporary of Gandon, the architect of Georgian Dublin.
So true is the parallel between them that it seems in
no way remarkable that Catherine should have
tried to negotiate with Gandon to come and work
in St. Petersburg. Quarenghi was no inspired
genius, but a competent grammarian, and an architect fit to be entrusted with the embellishment of an
Imperial capital.[1] Rossi, his successor, was born at

[1] The classical purity of his designs can be studied in a
book published after his death, on his return to Italy, by his
heirs (Milan, 1821). He was the last great architect of Italian
tradition.

Naples, his mother being an Italian ballerina, and his father a Russian. There had been Russian classical architects before Rossi: Sakharov, who built the Admiralty: and Voronikhin, architect of the Kazan Cathedral. The masterpiece of Rossi was the Michel Palace, built by Alexander I for his younger brother, and which elicited prodigies of admiration in its day. The front has a Corinthian portico of eight pillars; but it is more especially the interior that represents all that the Russian classical manner could accomplish. Floors inlaid with Carelian woods, and with rosewood, ebony, and mahogany; walls of scagliola, imitating the yellow Siena, shining mirrors, candelabra of Siberian jasper, pier tables of which the slabs are of opaque blue glass. Other rooms have walls of polished scagliola of a pure and dazzling white, with sky blue hangings; or imitation marble walls of a pigeon egg blue, highly polished, with eight columns at each end, of blue scagliola with gilt capitals. The curtains and their pelmets are designed by a master hand. They hang from light airy cornices, or in festoons and massive draperies which, drawn aside, display the marble walls painted with gilt arabesques, or, more simply, with cupids and wreaths of roses. This method of painting in oil and gold upon scagliola, and fixing the colours, was the invention of Italian craftsmen working under Rossi. In the first place it had been essential to find the alabaster needed for the composition of the scagliola, and this was eventually discovered in the government of Kazan. 'His Majesty the King of England (George IV)', we read, 'with that anxiety to promote the improvement of the elegant arts and exquisite taste for them, which have ever distinguished him, caused an application to be made, through the Russian Ambassador, for a specimen of the white scagliola, and the manner in which it is ornamented by gilding and painting in oil. A square block of a moderate size was prepared under the direction of Rossi, and painted by Scotti and Vighi. This specimen was inspected by the King, by whose command it was delivered over to Mr. Nash, who did not think favourably of it.' That scagliola was thus condemned by stucco is the illustration of that age; but, in St. Petersburg, this style of the Regency, as we would call it, reaches to its zenith. In no other city was it used upon so lavish a scale; and, of this, the Michel Palace is the conspicuous example. An exotic air breathes upon those apartments of sky blue or dazzling white, their mirrors multiplying without end and their gilded ceilings, when it is considered that this is Russia, that the snow makes brighter the plumage in the bird cages that hang in the windows, that the servants enter in long caftans and with slippered feet, that there are caviar and vodka on the zakuski table. Classical building has never been so artificial as in this city of the Tsars.

The Marble Palace was not less exotic in its day. This is of earlier date and one who saw it in its prime, in 1799, remarks of it: 'The prodigies of enchantment which we read of in the Tales of the Genii are here called forth into reality, and the temples raised by the luxuriant fancy of our poets may be considered as a picture of the marble palace which Jupiter, when the burden of cares drives him from heaven, might make his delightful abode.' This palace was built by Catherine for her favourite, Orlov, and was lived in by another of her lovers, Stanislaus Poniatowski, last king of Poland, in his exile. Grigori Orlov was the Jupiter of this Marble Palace, but he died too soon and his place was taken by the elegant and ineffectual Poniatowski. But that recent panegyric is no exaggeration if applied to the Taurida Palace. Its very name betrays its history: Taurida, or the Chersonese. When Potemkin conquered the Crimea this was his reward. Here her favourite and satrap beheld Catherine for the last time by the glitter of twenty thousand waxlights.

The building is of one storey, with a Doric portico. But the whole Taurida Palace is a multitude of pillars. You enter by the portico and find a colonnade in front of you, across the hall, of which the two central pillars have a wider space between them and lead into an immense vestibule or octagon, called the rotunda. A double range of Ionic columns leads into the ballroom. It is nearly a hundred yards long by thirty yards across, the two long sides each formed by an open double colonnade of Ionic pillars, thirty-five feet high, their shafts festooned with gold and silver wreaths, in imitation of the conqueror's laurel. Along the passage formed at each side of the room by the double row of columns there hang cut glass chandeliers, the lights of which are reflected in great mirrors. At each end, the room is circular, with great windows down to the ground, the side of the room opposite the entrance being a winter garden filled in its day, and on its winter nights, with camellias and orange trees. In another part of the Taurida there is a theatre, of which the parapet of the boxes is formed from solid cut crystal, with an arrangement to admit lights behind it, so as to throw a dazzling fire around the audience. The Taurida, obviously, has known the glitter of dia‑ monds. This ballroom was the scene of the last party given by Potemkin, who left the capital the next morning and died a few weeks later. In sober truth, the most gorgeous evening since the banquet of Trimalchio; but a spectacle more than a feast of gluttony.

For Potemkin, in character, was part Diaghilev, part Peter the Great. Who would not have seen him receive the Empress in the portico, as she got down from her coach, and lead her through the palace which she had built for him, but which the force of his personality had warmed from its chill classicism, into the glittering ballroom? How different the reality from how it would ever be represented in the cinema! Their personalities, because of some rumour of their splendour, have ever been the prey of nove‑ lists and scenario writers, but truth is safer left to the imagination than portrayed by actors. Potemkin was something of a Falstaff or a Hercules. His char‑ acter partook of both, but in the Russian or the

Tartar canon. He was one-eyed like the Cyclops;
and, as most giants, could be entranced by music.
In this he was different from his mistress, Catherine,
to whom it meant nothing, or was even painful. It
was a side of Russian character which she had not
assimilated; though it could be remarked that the
Germans were as fond of music as the Russians. As
for Potemkin, there is some evidence that he was in
negotiation with Mozart to come to Russia in the
capacity of court musician to himself, a project
which both their deaths prevented. Potemkin had
a wild, disordered fancy; and a personal quality, an
attack or touch, which can only be described as a
great hand in everything. He was original, by
instinct, and in all his acts. Grown to a great scale,
and proportioned to that. One of the huge physiques
of Russian history: to be ranked, though only for his
follies, with the Tsar Peter, the Patriarch Nicon, or
even with the great actor, Chaliapin. This scene we
are witnessing is the apotheosis of Potemkin. The
male favourites of an Elizabeth or a Catherine must
always be of more interest to the historian than a
Pompadour or du Barri. But Potemkin is the male
favourite of all history. When they tired of each
other, he chose her lovers for her. His letters to her,

strewn with the Russian diminutives, are the letters of a bear to a lioness, for this woman, who was not beautiful, nor an artist, breathed a greatness and a large mind, of a feline pride, in all her acts and deeds. Not born to her position, but rather choosing it by force, she must remain, despite all changes of historical opinion, among the greatest women there have ever been. Her achievements were so conspicuous that her venality, only reversed in rôle from that of Charles II or of Louis XV, passed without censure, even in the censorious Victorian age. She was succeeded by a mad son, almost certainly the child of Saltykov, her lover, and not a Romanov at all. He, in his turn, was murdered with the connivance of his eldest son. And yet the Russian monarchy continued for another hundred years, and more. This is due, entirely, to Catherine and to the transmission of her genius to the second generation, missing the madman Paul.

The visual or objective side of her life portrays the Northern Semiramis in a background that was half-classical, half-barbaric. This was perfect in detail, down to the jewelled handles of her walking sticks. It is even present in the accounts of her in the gardens of Tsarskoe Selo surrounded by her troop

of English greyhounds; or with her Russian borzois.
She brought their shallow pates and high-bred, thin
limbs for the first time into history. In her relations
with Potemkin she was, at first, infatuated, and then
fond; never in many years tiring of their friendship
or becoming bored. 'The Prince of Taurida', she
wrote upon his death, 'was the most extraordinary
man who has ever lived'; and he had, certainly, a
primitive force which was rare in the powdered
century in which he lived. He is reputed to have had
powers of mimicry amounting to genius, while his
multiple energies are proved within a small sphere by
his successive romances with three sisters who were
his nieces. Some premonition may have affected him
upon this last evening in St. Petersburg. He was
fifty-four years old, and worn out by his contradictions. The ballroom of the Taurida Palace will
have been thronged with figures as lively as in a
masquerade. Their likelihood can be tested in the
portraits by Levitzky (1735–1822).[1] He painted a

[1] The portrait painter Levitzky is the subject of the only
book ever published by Serge de Diaghilev: *Russian Painting
of the Eighteenth Century*. Vol. I., D. G. Levitzky. This was
published in 1902, and contains reproductions of 121 portraits. Levitzky was a serf, and his name would suggest that
he was a Jew.

great number, perhaps a hundred or more, of the personalities assembled in this ballroom. But there is no good portrait of the host, Potemkin. Catherine and the Prince of Taurida must have sat, side by side, at supper. All we know is that, on leaving, as she reached the door, Potemkin fell on his knees and burst into tears. It was their farewell. The ballroom was closed. In later times the Taurida Palace was occupied by the widow of the murdered Paul I, by various others, and then by superannuated ladies of the Imperial Court. Now, it must have different tenants. But may still be haunted.

A curious interlude in the history of the Taurida Palace was the vast Russian art exhibition organized there by Serge de Diaghilev in 1905, and consisting of more than three thousand paintings. Special rooms were devoted to Catherine the Great, and to Paul I, whose mad features much impressed the public. This was in Diaghilev's 'World of Art' period, before he became interested in the ballet. He had travelled all over Russia to collect the pictures from provincial governors and country landowners. In an article in his paper he refers to the Russian paintings still to be found scattered about the Im⁄perial Palaces, 'whose wealth of art treasures is be⁄

yond imagination'. 'The Alexander III Museum',
he continues, 'without making a single purchase
from any individual could in this way possess thirty-
nine of the best works of Levitzky.' And he goes on
to suggest that all old masters and works of art be
collected from the Chinese Gallery in the Gatchina
Palace, the Treasury of the Ministry of the Imperial
Court, the Moscow Armoury, the Academy of
Science, the Academy of Arts, the Holy Synod, the
Alexander-Nevsky Monastery, and the Roumiant-
zov Museum.[1] More especially, as we have said, it
was the room devoted to Paul I in this exhibition
that impressed all who saw it. A kind of madness
of a Russian sort lurked in his Kalmuck features
and his aggressive eyes. In his youth, as the Comte
du Nord, he had travelled to the Court of Louis
XVI, and to Venice, where the banquets and
regattas held in his honour by the Serenissima in its
decline were painted by Guardi. He was half-mad
already, and spent more than seven hours visiting
the Arsenal of Venice. It showed itself in an insane
degree of interest in military technique, and an
ambition to be Tsar Peter and Frederick the Great

[1] Cf. *Diaghilev*, by Serge Lifar, Putnam & Co., London,
1940, p. 142.

at once. He put the Russian army into Prussian
uniforms; and in advance of some modern dic-
tators prescribed a regulation dress for all. His was
the form of lunacy which seeks to prove that it is
normal by a mad show of energy, in little things.
But as Russian in his madness as the Tsar Peter in
his greatness. Mad son of a great mother: but pro-
genitor of two great men, Alexander and Nicholas.
An insane episode, because it was so pointless, was
when he accepted to be Grand Prior of Malta, after
the expulsion of the order by Napoleon in 1798. The
exiled Knights were invited to St. Petersburg, and
there are relics of this fantasy on ceilings in the
Michael Palace (where he was soon murdered),
painted with the revival of the Order; and in a
church and priory built in the park at Gatchina, to
the designs of Quarenghi, where the Knights assembled under the presidency of the mad Emperor.
His portrait was painted in the Grand Prior's robes;
but it was all the toy or plaything of a madman.
Yet this mad interval between three great reigns is
as typical of Russian history as their whole achieve-
ment. It is the clown's turn: a parody done by the
idiot and, in symbol, the destructive force of all the
ignorance and atavism in the Russian soil.

In the words of Diaghilev the wealth of art treasures in the Imperial Palaces was beyond description. More could be said of the architecture of the capital. It is a city of Grecian porticos. We could begin, even, with the Imperial Mews, of which the back, along the Moika canal, presents a piazza of the order of Paestum, with a church in the centre of the façade belonging to the Mews, the work of an Italian architect, Trombara. It is a stone or stuccoed building of a delicate and unsoiled white tint. Or we should mention the Exchange, with its peristyle of Doric columns round it, designed by Thomas de Thomon, standing on a granite quay with steps down to the water; and its pair of granite rostral columns a hundred feet in height, decorated with bronze prows of ships, in honour of Mercury, and each surmounted by figures of Atlas bearing a hollow globe in which fires are lit for solemn occasions. So many porticoes. But how much of mystery in the Imperial Palaces! What, for instance, is the Chinese Gallery at Gatchina mentioned by Diaghilev? Has it a Chinese bridge with a balustrade of imitation coral on which sit four stone Chinamen with their parasols? Is it part of the palace: or in the park and one of the

## PAVILIONS IN THE PARK

Arcadian wonders? There are so many such at Peterhof and Tsarskoe Selo.[1] So many pavilions, from Rastrelli downwards; some of them most fanciful, in the shape of a five-pointed star, with a domed hall and five wings, all standing on a stone island in the water. Hermitages and heathen temples, interiors exquisite in their contents, of which the keys are always lost, or everyone is too tired, already, to take another step, for there is no fatigue to be compared to that of seeing palaces. And it may be winter and two feet of snow. We may have to plough with our sledges through the winter plain. These pavilions, which in other countries are mere summer houses, have here the dimensions of small palaces. In this winter evening it is an enchantment to think of them, for some will be quite lost in the falling snowflakes. You could drive in your sledge, at random, and come to a pavilion where everything has been sleeping for a hundred years,

[1] Many of these are illustrated from contemporary engravings, or from photographs, in *Gli Architetti Italiani in Russia*, by Ettore Lo Gatto, 1935, etc.: a series published by the Italian Government. The first volume deals with Italian buildings in Moscow and its vicinity; the second is devoted to Rastrelli, Trombara, Quarenghi, and others, working at St. Petersburg and in its neighbourhood.

but the clocks are still wound, the tiled stoves are lit.

Or we can look, for the last time, upon the country palace of the Sleeping Beauty. It is twelve hundred feet, or nearly a quarter of a mile in length, with three floors in which to search for her. This is how it runs. The chapel is at the left extremity with its five gold domes. There is a flight of eleven windows; a more important portion, in advance, with nine; then a flight of eleven; the central member with seventeen; eleven more; then nine projecting; and eleven more. And the whole façade is alive with gilded statues. The roof line has a crowd of them, between gilt vases. Enormous golden caryatids stand by each ground floor window, so that every approach is guarded by a giant at either side. This stupendous scene painting, for it is that more than architecture, partakes of the fabulous seen obliquely from an angle, owing to the counterpoint of these same caryatids, seen one after another, and the projecting portions coming forward in their rhythm. A great architect might have not succeeded. This façade is wonderful because it is unreal. There is, even, a primary quality in the gargantuan proportion; that same quality which affects the imagina tion in the Farnese Hercules, and in the garden statues of Villa Lante and Caprarola; the sleeping river gods, the lichened Faunus, giants who slumber in their blocks of stone, but have a mortality of their own, having no connection with the sculptor. These caryatids are in descent from the mute gods of Vignola, but have become ogres or Atlantes of a fairy story, come down through comedy, having forsaken Virgilian woods and lily-silvered vales. For the palace is painted in pantomime colours. It has green walls: the columns or pilasters are white: every statue, pedestal, and capital is gilded. So are —or were—the vases, carvings, and other orna-ments. All rising out of the snow. Quite empty and deserted. A flight of a hundred windows in a line, three times over, one above another, to the vases and statues upon the parapet. For this is the façade that looks out upon the gardens. And every gilded out-line has a shade of snow upon it, that follows it exactly, like the bevelling upon a mirror, or a shadow drawing. The gilded sashes of the windows, in square panes of glass, give an effect as though this sleeping palace was part glass, itself. There will be miracles of frost flowers upon those windows, and they will be impossible to look through. But, once again, all the clocks will be ticking. Time moves on, and the idle days are numbered. There is no other sign of life. We walk right round the palace until we find the Colonnade of Cameron, one of the won׳ders of Tsarskoe Selo, being the addition of a hang׳ing garden, a Palladian bridge that leads nowhere, to this vast total of follies and apartments. It is too, the masterwork of Charles Cameron, a work of genius in the Palladian style of England, yet trans׳muted by some curious magic, for it is more than that. The Gallery of Tsarskoe Selo consists of an Ionic colonnade, not far from the body of the palace, and raised on a large terrace. It contains an oblong room in which Catherine dined in the summer, and an aerial garden. It is quite probable that this colon׳nade and hanging garden were built, half seriously and half in jest, as an allusion to her being the Semiramis of the North.

But in the snow, and, indeed, in summer too, something even in the elegance and grace of the building, perhaps the fact that it is raised on its high terrace, recalls the prints and pictures of Russian fairs. Montagnes russes, the first mountain railways of the fairs, had to have a raised building at each end, a tower from which the slide or switchback took its start, and these were often given pillars and porticoes, with carved figures of dancers of the fair upon their side walls. By some transformation or meta⁄morphosis, for it has no real structural resemblance, and may be due more to the colours in the sky or to some quite extraneous reason, the Colonnade of Tsarskoe Selo is not a hanging garden but a mon⁄tagne russe—in imitation—for it has no action, no switchback, it is the summer dining room of Semi⁄ramis, yet, like all things Russian, it is Russian in total and in detail, and could be nothing else. We are to imagine Catherine dining in this Colonnade, her Russian elkhounds round her, her ambitions pointing her towards the Hellespont, with so much that is Oriental or Asiatic in the contradiction of these classic columns and the Tartar soil or sub⁄stratum of her revenues. Syllables of the Russian tongue sound odd in this landscape of an Arcadian park, seen through the pillars. Today, on this winter afternoon, the flying colonnade of Tsarskoe Selo is like the Rialto if the Grand Canal ran dry. Seen from below, it looks stranded in a pale green sky: a bridge, a colonnade, a pleasure barge, left empty in a long winter. We come back to the palace, as snow begins to fall again. But the snow has begun

III

to have black shadows. They are torn and sinister,
black as a crow, so that the snow on the window-
sills is as stained as in a London fog. The whole
immense palace, like the frigate in an old engraving
of an Arctic expedition, is engulfed or laid up in the
snow. The crew have left it. We cannot look in
through the frozen windows. Within, there are
rooms that are like cabinets of tortoiseshell or amber,
floored with rare woods, with golden doorways and
mirrors magnifying the perspective. The enfilade
runs, for ever, on three floors in the double or
parallel line of both façades, broken or interrupted
by the staircases that are triumphal ascents, and
should be but painted scenes leading to more canvas
splendours, but are, here, actual and real. Listen?
You may hear the booted step of Zoritch, her
hussar lover; the high voice of Lanskoy; some-
one mimicking Potemkin. But our thoughts are
more impersonal. We look for the secret or spirit
of this sleeping palace, and will not find it behind locked doors. We will look for it at the ball,
tonight.

The entire lights of the capital burn as though lit
by a single hand. This is Russia as the Russians
loved it, not so long ago. It is as Russian as Alabiev's

*Nightingale*.[1] How quickly that gives the character!
For those who do not know that little tune, how is
it to be described? It is a body or synthesis of the
Russian day or night, not by association, but in the
tune itself, which is trite and ridiculous, and could
be formed of air and water, or of bread and salt
offered in the Russian manner. At the door of a
house, to make the house your own. *The Nightingale*
is Russian in its taste and smell. Its little clockwork
mechanism lasts but for a moment, and builds up
the image. As Russian as another phrase of music
can be Italian, tasting of the South, touched on the
lutes or mandolines. This is a sledge song: music of
the troikas: or of the tiled stove when the double
windows keep out the cold. It is every Russian
custom and tradition. A nightingale in the wood of
birch trees, when the spring flowers begin, and
there are gilded domes and cupolas not far away, in
a provincialism that has no frontiers in space or
time. There is singing down by the river, in the
sunset. And where does the river run? Out of
Europe into Tartary, till it is lost in the nomad vastness. That little song, or microcosm, is a picture of

---

[1] This song, composed by an amateur, was often sung by
Rosina during the music lesson in *The Barber of Seville*.

this immense capital with its million souls, for its image or sentiment is universal in them, and does not alter from end to end of a whole continent. They all know, and understand, its simple meaning. It has the same values for them all. It is implicit in the cold winds that blow from the Neva, down the quays of granite. The droshky or the sledge driver could sing this song. It is not peculiar to the troika along the country roads; but is sung at the opera, and upon the islands in the summer evenings.

How personal and unforgettable is that first understanding of the Russian idiom in music! Apart from little things, in the writer's instance it was Mussorgsky's *Khovantchina*, when fourteen years old. From a stall at the right-hand side of the orchestra, where the brass instruments were playing. To be told this was a drunken genius, and be shown his portrait, that of a drunken monk out of his own opera; and listen to the declamation, which is Shakespearian in its impressiveness and sense of tragedy. This was, of course, Rimsky-Korsakov's edition of *Khovantchina*. How much more wonderful must it be in the original, in which Rimsky-Korsakov thought the orchestration was so uncouth and clumsy! His neat, desk manner has tidied it too

much. But who would know this in the first intoxication! The blare and frenzy of the Persian dances;
the stabbing of a man who wore a high white bearskin cap; the burning of the Raskolniki or Old
Believers; now and then an aria for a woman,
probably a wedding song or nursery song, in its
Slav sort of freshness which is never that of flower
or fruit but fresh like a mushroom, come out of the
soil, not from the rain and air; fresh like a crayfish
from the clayey brook; like the tall sunflower near
the house, if a flower at all; like the beetroot field;
like the Northern berries in the dank autumnal
wood; of such, or such, it is in simile; never of the
rose, or vineyard, or the summer seas. The same
character pervades all Russian music. We hear it in
the opening of *Le Sacre du Printemps*, in a theme that
argues or contradicts its own simplicity, but presents, none the less, the familiar scene in an archaic
setting. It is a Stone Age, but the very megaliths are
Russian. The ancestors are from the steppe, where
the rivers run into the Black Sea or the Caspian.
In *Khovantchina* their eyes and cheekbones are no
different; nor the pallor of the true Slav. These are
the Russians, who are the Antipodes to all other
nations, born, it would seem, into a different per-

spective or proportion, often overtaken by disaster owing to ignorance and vastness, but wrongly blamed for never having been happy. They are the mute animal upon whom experiments are made, of one kind and another of innoculation. Disease may, or may not, have taken; but illness, if it is not mortal, has a term of years.

We cannot believe that it was its wickedness that struck it down. Poverty was appalling in the big towns, but it was the misery of African or Oriental cities. With this difference, the aching cold. Such conditions could not continue close to the European order. And, perhaps, it was more dangerous in the wide prospects and open spaces of a modern capital. In the muddy lanes, among the wooden tenements of an older world, life was less heartless. There was more of human company than in a capital that was laid out upon too large a scale, even, for its million population, and that in the same wide street, eternal to walk along, one street, from Bond Street to the Mile End Road, ended in shacks and hovels. However, for many, if not for most, snow on the roofs and street is a soft covering, something which makes the winter pretty. Tonight, in the year we see it, this is how many would remember it from their childhood.

This was the reality they loved, and that was their home. This is the vision that has been taken from them, for more poverty and a more enslaving servitude. No need to foresee that. It hides at the wind-rubbed corner, on the façade of granite, and in the nameless, dosshouse cellar. It will come. And it is better not to think of it. Nothing could have prevented it. Or so it is better to believe. But behold this city that glitters in the snow! There are persons still living who were little babes tonight. Or, even, can remember this winter, of many winters, and how warm it was at home. They sleigh, every evening, and bring back the parcels. It is the little world of mothers and governesses. One evening, among many evenings, of the interminable years. But the Christmas snow is not only for the children. All the world drives in sledges. No one talks of poverty. The beggars are professional, as in Eastern cities. Tonight is tonight: and tomorrow will be just the same. Why waste a moment of it! It is our's, and your's, to spend. In the winter this city only lives at night. And in the summer, too. Tonight there is the ball. In less than an hour, in a few moments, it will begin. It is time to get ready. It is time to go upstairs. The candles are lit upon the dressing table. The stove gives out its warmth. The sleigh waits at the door.

As we get nearer, driving through the great arch of the État Major, the entire Winter Palace comes into view blazing with lights from every window. The horses' hooves sound loud in the archway, and more and more of the endless palace unrolls in per⁄spective, in front across the square. Carriages and sledges come in from every direction and make for different entrances, the stream of all that silent traffic being broken by the Alexander Column, a huge monolith of granite with a statue of an arch⁄angel a hundred and fifty feet into the air, and great braziers burning at its foot. The polished granite looks so cold; but, turning back, the great archway, behind, and the advancing wings of the État Major, so immense in scale, enclose the square and seem to shelter the coachmen and footmen who warm them⁄selves at the braziers, and watch more sleighs arriv⁄ing and the glittering lights. We are half⁄way across the square, passing other sledges that have their har⁄ness covered with blue netting in order that the snow shall not blow back upon the dresses for the ball. At this moment the whole bulk of the palace, with its three storeys, rises up like a ship before a rowing boat. The further windows, at both ends, lose their separate illumination and flatten out into one great whole that lies to either side, and high above. There is an advancing portion, with a porch in which we wait for the sledge in front to drop its passengers, and drive away. This is the Ambassador's entrance. There are four other entrances. Grand Dukes come in by the Saltykov: Court officials by the Imperial: Civil officials by the Jurdan: military officers by the Commander's. Court servants come forward and take the coats and furs. We are at the foot of the great staircase, the Escalier des Ambassadeurs, with wide and shallow steps of marble, thickly carpeted, and climbing in two flights. Upon the four other staircases, at different ends of the palace, it is the same. Every step is crowded, and the guests climb slowly into the golden halls above.

But we must begin our acquaintance with the particular inhabitants of the Winter Palace. In the hall at the foot of the staircase, on duty at the others, too, are Grenadiers of the Golden Guard of the Palace. This is a special body, a full company in strength, who post the sentries at the Alexander Column, and guard the room in which Nicholas I

died. They are his creation, and wear the uniform
he designed for them. Picked for their great height,
out of all the regiments who wore the Russian bearskin in the various European armies, these, in the
land of their invention, are the most gorgeous of the
whole creation. The Grenadiers of the Winter
Palace in a golden travesty of the bear hunters from
the Ural mountains.

Outside, at the Alexander Column, they wear
long grey coats. Here, they are in gala uniform.
White trousers, which button from knee downwards into their boots, so that only the black toe of
the boot is visible, and the effect is white trousers,
and white spats or leggings. A black tunic, cut like
a tight waistcoat with a breast of gold braid edged
with red, with red and golden cuffs and collars, a
golden bandolier crossed in front but carried in two
broad golden bands straight down their backs to
the cut-away tails, gold lined with red, upon which
is fastened a cartridge case embossed with a golden
double-headed eagle. They carry a sword at their
side, and a musket and fixed bayonet. Their musicians, who are on duty, too, have more elaborate
golden sleeves. But the chief feature is the enormous
bearskin kalpack, immensely high and bulky, with

a golden headpiece and a golden chain looped through it, with a golden grenade at the back, in symbol, and in front, a golden tassel hanging by the ear. They are on duty in a hall which is entirely of this period; the walls are gold and lapis lazuli, with a painted vase of blue and gold against a marbled panel, great doors with golden ornaments, and a red and gold carpet. They are shown, thus, in our frontispiece. To the top of their kalpacks may be as much as eight feet high, or nearly as much, and they are really formidable and magnificent with the golden ornaments upon the glossy bearskin. But they are attached, in particular, to the ground floor of the palace, the first line, as it were, of its gala defences, their bearskins being appropriate to the falling snow outside, and more impressive for being worn indoors against this Regency interior. And we continue up the marble staircase into the line of glittering halls.

Cossacks of the Guard in their scarlet uniforms, sword in hand, stand in two ranks and the guests move on between them, through room after room, till the flow from the other staircases joins in with them, and we reach the St. George's Hall, the Throne Room, the White Chamber and the gallery where the Corps Diplomatique are waiting. The

procession is already forming. It is the important
moment in the whole ceremony. For the ball has
not begun. There has been no music yet. Our dis-
embodiment, which lets us move freely where we
will, seeing everything, but invisible ourselves, has
this advantage that we need not enter into conver-
sation. We study the inhabitants of this world of
candle light, for every room has the glitter of many
hundreds of wax lights, and choose the peculiar and
significant.

All the ladies of the Court wear the 'Russian'
dress, of white silk, cut low with a close fitting
bodice and red velvet train, gold embroidered, and
the kokoshnik of red velvet and gold braid, like that
worn by nurses and peasant women, only more
sumptuous, diadem shaped, with a soft veil hanging
from it. The jewels are astonishing.[1] Other ladies,
who do not hold Court appointments, wear different colours, but always the long train and the

[1] General Mossolov mentions, at a later day, those of
Countess Shouvolova, Countess Vorontzova Dashkova,
Countess Sheremetyevskaya, Princess Kotchubey, Princess
Youssopova, and the pigeon egg emeralds of Madame Zino-
viev, wife of the Marshal of the Nobility of St. Petersburg.
These took the form of jewelled buttons to her 'Russian
dress'.

kokoshnik. There is the distinction, so like a fairy story, between the Dames à portrait and those who wear the monogram. The Dames à portrait, middle aged or old women, have a miniature of the Czarina framed in diamonds upon the left side of their bodice, which is esteemed a great honour; while the Demoiselles d'honneur have but the Imperial monogram set in diamonds. Ruby velvet is the colour worn by the Demoiselles d'honneur; while the Dames du palais, not always Dames à portrait, wear olive green. In addition, all the Grand Ducal families have their distinctive colours worn by their Duchesses and ladies-in-waiting: some, white and silver, rose, turquoise blue, or cornflower blue. There are Court ladies wearing the blue ribbon of the Order of St. Catherine with its diamond cross. In all this galaxy the Dames à portrait, with the miniatures upon their bodices, look like personages come down from the Contes de Perrault.

There are not many beauties among this large assembly. As with the original and authentic Russian ballet, from the Imperial School, the dancers are seldom beautiful. They were part of the whole scheme, not to be noticed individually, and so it is tonight. There are, however, those two contrasting types of Russians, men and women; those who from their eyes and bone formation, or from their colouring, could be nothing else than Russian; and those who, handsome or otherwise, could pass for any other race. A Dame à portrait here and there, could come from Marly or Versailles: another, or some other lady, is the Muscovite of legend.

But the procession is nearly formed. This is, in fact, the great ceremony of the Winter Palace, taking place upon other occasions of religious import, when the Imperial family proceed, in state, through the palace to the chapel; and process back again. Tonight it is no less of a ritual. But it is the opening of the ball. A pair of great halls is given over to the ceremony. First comes the Concert Room. Into this those persons are allowed to enter who have the peculiar right of 'going past the Chevalier Gardes'. A number of this regiment are posted at the doorway, in their white tunics and silver helms and breastplates, sword in hand, and the privilege consisted in being allowed to approach nearer than their persons to the sovereign. Beyond, lies the Malachite Room, into which only members of the Imperial family are allowed. The door of this room is guarded by Court Arabs.

## COURT ARABS

This special corps is as romantic in origin as the peyks or tressed halberdiers of the Grand Seraglio. They are termed Arabs because that is the old Russian name for all coloured men. In actual fact they are gigantic negroes. They wear white turbans and are dressed, à l'Oriental, in blue and red, subtly differenced, so that their long coats and baggy trousers and the silken scarves across their shoulders are never identical, but belong to the same scheme of colours. They wear Turkish slippers, and remain completely silent. These are no mere negroes: they are Christian Abyssinians. In the first place, in the eighteenth century, they will have been recruited as Court blackamoors who belonged to the Eastern Church. The exact time is uncertain, but it was probably in the reign of the Empress Elizabeth (1741–1761). Under Catherine the Great and her successors the Court Arabs became an intimate symbol of the Romanov ambitions. We may see in them, and they existed until 1917, the designs of Catherine upon Constantinople, and the reasons for which her second grandson was christened Constantine; the project, also, of Alexander I, at Tilsit, to divide the world into East and West for himself and Napoleon. Under Nicholas I, when they might have been abolished, the Court Arabs were maintained. This guard of Christian negroes in the Winter Palace, like an image borrowed from Byzantium, shadow every move against the Turkish Sultans. In the Crimean war; and, as we see them tonight, in times yet to come, when Alexander III liberated the Christians of the Balkans and his troops were encamped upon the Bosphorus in 1878. The unity of all Christian nations of the Eastern Church was the project, Slavs and Greeks among them; and, in a dream, it might include Copts and Ethiopians. They are stage extras, hired negroes standing against the painted wings of Bakst or Benois; but do not mistake them! They come down to us from the golden age of the theatre, contem-porary with Bibiena, and these playthings of the Russian Court, in an age of rococo, have their sig-nificance.

There is more of the Court Arabs that an enquir-ing mind would seek to know. In later times, in this present reign of Alexander II, they are recruited by the Russian Consul in Ethiopia, and, before that, by some diplomatic agent. They must be Christian negroes, of the negro type, not the Hamitic Ethio-pian, who is aquiline and with a straight mop of hair. They live in the Winter Palace, and are taken, in summer, to Tsarskoe Selo. Do they return to Abyssinia? May there be Court Arabs, in 1941, who went back to their country after the revolution, and if they could be found, having learnt no Russian, could recall being on guard at the door of the Malachite Room when the polonaise was about to begin? How remote this would sound, interpreted, upon the shores of Lake Tana, where there are Christian monasteries and the Blue Nile rises! Or at Gondar, not far away, with its Portuguese ruins from the reign of Prester John! They would remember the Neva frozen into solid blocks of ice, the falling snowflakes, and the interior splendour. The back staircases, and the attics below the roof, whence they looked out upon the Northern capital. How were they brought from Ethiopia to St. Petersburg? How many Court Arabs were there? It is impossible to know. At the coronation of Alexander II, in 1856, eight 'nègres de la cour' walked in the procession: at that of Nicholas II, in 1896, their number was reduced to four. An English account of the marriage of the Tsarewitch (Alexander III), in 1866, to the sister of Queen Alexandra, describes a banquet in the Winter Palace at which there were covers for 2,200 guests, and a lacquey standing behind every chair. The banquet was followed by a ball. 'At twelve the supper rooms were thrown open. During the meal the Imperial party were surrounded by a number of black Mame-lukes, who were on duty for the occasion.' This has the sound of more than eight Court Arabs; and perhaps there may have been as many as twenty, or more, at their full strength. In that immense book which illustrates the coronation of Alexander II they are to be seen, at the banquet, handing round wines and refreshments. Six or eight are on duty at the entrance to the Malachite Room. And their function, so near to the Imperial family, past the picket of Chevalier Gardes in the next room, makes them more than ever like guardians of the Grand Seraglio.

But the ball is about to begin. The Masters of Ceremonies are grouped at the door, each with his wand of office, a long staff of ebony ending in an ivory ball with a two-headed eagle perched upon it, and a bow of bright blue silk tied in the St. Andrew's knot. At a sign from the Grand Marshal they strike their wands three times upon the floor. Upon the third stroke, the Court Arabs, from both sides, fling wide the doors. The orchestra begins the polonaise. The Grand Marshal, with the Masters of Ceremonies behind him, precedes the Tsar, wand in hand, clearing the way before him, and the entire procession emerges from the Malachite Room. The giant Tsarewitch comes behind his father; and, after him, his four brothers, the Grand Dukes Vladimir, Alexis, Serge, and Paul, all men of great height. In the words of a contemporary: 'Amongst a nation certainly not remarkable for good looks, the Princes of the House of Romanov are conspicuous for their stature and kingly appearance; if the Russian people had to choose a Tsar on the same system as the children of Israel chose Saul, there are not, I think, many families in the Empire who would stand a better chance of election than the descendants of Rurik.' The Tsarina and the wife of the Tsarewitch take part in the polonaise with their husbands; the latter wearing a silver kokoshnik that is on fire with diamonds, great ropes of pearls, and the triple diamond necklace which was one of the marriage presents given to her by the Tsar. The other Grand Duchesses wear rubies, sapphires, or emeralds, that match the colour of their dresses. Three times the cortège passes up and down the room, while the orchestra plays overhead along the gallery. At the end of each turn they change partners. It is not a dance, exactly. But the pace is more rhythmic and regular than that of walking.

It is the polonaise from *A Life for the Tsar*, by Glinka. A Russian polonaise which is a little different from the Polish. To our ears, it has to sound a strange, barbaric march. We could not be accustomed, yet, to Russian music. But how fortunate and typical are the Russians in the mere name of their 'primitive' of music! Glinka! In sound, it is military music in an unfamiliar key; and when you repeat his name it is a music of trumpets and kettledrums, ending shrilly; or like a military march or dance that employs the cymbals, that is à la Cosaque, in strange time and rhythm, ending unexpectedly, with a dying ring, an echo in the metal. Glinka, once more! Listen to his two syllables! The name has onomatopoeia in it. An Ukrainian name, we will suppose, but it has the sound of brass and cymbals to it, with a dancing rhythm. The light shrill music of a mounted band. The music of this polonaise is set and formal, not romantic like a polonaise of Chopin, and with another fire, not of rebellion. It is odd and peculiar, in Cossack or

Circassian rhythm, in harmony, therefore, with many of the figures round us whom as yet there has been scarcely time to study. But, above all, this music has none of the Russian melancholy. Could we compare it, while listening to it, with the polo-naise from the Polish scene of *Boris Godunov*, we would know that sinister preluding and its foretaste of tragedy to come. This, on the other hand, is of peasant loyalties; and in the ballroom of the Winter Palace its images call to mind platoons or beds of military planted in their rows, as in the reign of Nicholas I, and those wonders that it was supposed the liberation of the serfs would bring. Who could think, tonight, that Alexander II, the liberator, who leads the polonaise, will, one day, lie murdered in the snow! Its music, wild and barbaric as it may be, is so confident and patriotic for the future.

After it comes a mazurka, and the dancing is general. There is time to look round. We see hussar officers in white and gold: 'en dolman blanc, soutaché d'or et fourré d'une bordure de zibeline'. It sounds better, thus, in French ; tirailleurs in ma-genta shirts and dark green fur-trimmed tunics; officers from the Caucasus in long white coats. In-numerable Court gentlemen in gold-braided coats:

Court chamberlains in blue frockcoats stiff with
gold. Count Mossolov mentions, in a later generation, the 'national costumes of the Hungarian Magnates. The gold-embroidered kuntush, or Polish
dress, of Marquis Vielopolski and Marquis Gon-
zago-Myskowsky, from Russian Poland; and the
beshmets of the Caucasian nobles, shod in tchu-
viaks, or mocassins, in which they danced without
a sound.' Tonight it is more varied still, for a ball
under Alexander II, such as this, at which there
are seven to eight thousand guests, never took place
under his successors. This was the year in which the
Russian armies entered Samarkand. Tashkent was
already taken. We see the Khans of Central Asia in
their snow-white turbans; and others in national
costumes, or brocaded gowns patterned with great
formal flowers, whose identity is unknown even to
most Russians at the ball, so lately have they sub-
mitted and been given Russian status. They are
Musulmans, and may come from Khiva or Bo-
khara. There are Tartars and Siberian Cossacks.
But, also, the Caucasus was newly conquered. An
old man, tall, and with a hooked nose like a
scimitar, in a white cashmere robe and wearing an
immense white turban, is Schamyl, the hero of the

Caucasus. Young Circassians are to be seen in long close-fitting coats and high sheepskin hats, black or white, rising above the crowd, like the hats in Persian miniatures of the seventeenth century. They come from Transcaucasia, bordering on the Caspian. The Christian princes of the Caucasus gave up their kingdoms and were ennobled by the Tsar. There are the princes of Imeretia and the Bagrations. Georgia itself, and Tiflis its capital, was of old, Iberia, where the dynasty of the Bagratides reigned from the eighth century until 1801, the oldest reigning family in Europe, and claiming descent from King David. The last king was Heraclius, who willed his kingdom to the Tsar. Conspicuous among the Georgian and Circassian nobles are members of the family of Dadian, former rulers of Mingrelia, who surrendered their principality in 1867. The princesses of their family, famed for their beauty, had such names as Salomé; and both male and female, the particular title of Dédophiles of Mingrelia.

After more mazurkas the time has come for supper. The Imperial family lead the way into the supper room preceded by Masters of Ceremonies armed with their wands. They sit, with backs to the wall, in strict precedence of rank, at a supper table raised upon a platform. None but those who wear the blue ribbon of the Order of St. Andrew can be seated at their table. Three or four hundred persons have their supper in this room, by invitation, and sitting twelve at a table in two long rows; but they are round tables, and an orange tree, a palm, or a camellia brought from the hothouse, rises from the middle of each table, its boards being placed over the cask or tub with an opening to allow for the stem. In the other supper rooms the long tables are ornamented in the same way with palms and flowering trees. It is the custom for the Tsar to walk about in the main supper room, from table to table, talking to the guests. A place is left empty for him at the tables where it has been arranged that he should sit, and behind each empty chair a skorok-hod is standing. When the Tsar has finished talking the skorokhod makes a sign to the gentlemen-in-waiting, who come up to him, and precede him to the next table. If this is well managed, without nervousness, it is a great pantomime of courtly manners; and Alexander II is the person for it. He has the great height of his own family, so often referred to, and shared collaterally with his Prussian cousins, the Emperor William I and the Emperor Frederick, for his own grandmother, Alexandra Feodorowna, wife of Paul I, was daughter of Frederick William III, of Prussia. He has something, therefore, of Prussian military bearing, and through his father, Nicholas I, an inheritance of the good looks of Queen Louise of Prussia, and enough sanity with it to balance the madness of Paul I. But, withal, Alexander is very Russian. It could be, or not, the blood of Saltykov; for, if not, if Saltykov was not the lover of Catherine and father of Paul I, then there is nothing Russian in the Romanovs. But that is hardly credible in the presence of so many of the family. They could be nothing but Muscovite, for good or evil.

Who, and what, then are the skorokhods? They are Court runners or running footmen; another fantasy from the Court of King Florestan, come down from the Middle Ages, but surviving in the Winter Palace until the Revolution.[1] A skorokhod, it will

[1] Running footmen were in existence at Naples under the Bourbon kings. They appeared in the royal procession, every 8th September, in the Festa of Piedigrotta. 'In honour of the day all the available troops of the Kingdom, amounting generally to thirty thousand men, are marched into the city, and line the long street of the Chiaja. . . . About four o'clock

be remembered, called in the morning with the invitation. They run before the Tsar's coach to clear a way for it, though its progress is at a walking pace, but it is the tradition that they must learn the particular gait, half-walking and half-running, which is expected of them, and which is achieved by a peculiar step and a motion of the arms, in fact, a mime or dumb show of hurrying through a crowded street. They are dressed for running, that is to say, they wear knee breeches and light shoes; but their costume in other respects, too, is distinctive and original. It has become formalized, so that it is known, at once, though the reasons for it have long been lost in time. Once more, this is the Russian equivalent of the Contes de Perrault, a legend from mediaeval chivalry transmuted through the living fantasies of Le Roi Soleil, but transplanted long ago into Russian soil. As with the Court Arabs, we do not know their number. At the coronation

His Majesty (Ferdinand II) and the Royal Family, in their state carriages, and escorted by flying footmen, set out in procession. Each prince drives in a separate carriage. The coachmen, and footmen too, are without hats, but wear full-bottomed powdered wigs, a relic of Spanish etiquette.' Cf. Octavian Blewitt's *Guide to Naples*, 1853, p. 113 *et seq*. Their characteristic walk can be seen in old prints of this procession.

of Alexander II, six 'coureurs en grand panache' walked in the procession: forty years later, when Nicholas II was crowned at Moscow, only four 'coureurs' took part. From their complicated duties as messengers in the palace, and up and down the capital, and the frequent mention of them in all descriptions of the Court, as though they were a conspicuous feature of it, their number must have been more considerable than that. At one time they were in attendance not only at the Winter Palace but at Gatchina, Tsarskoe Selo, and other palaces. Gatchina, as already stated, was largely built by Paul I, who established the exiled Knights of Malta in the park. After his death it was the residence of Alexandra Feodorowna, his widow. An English man who went there in 1828, driven in a sledge from the capital across the snow, concludes, unctuously: 'Her Majesty having condescended to send orders for that purpose, we partook of a magni ficent repast in one of the dining rooms of the palace, served up by a number of Imperial footmen and couriers of the Court, whom I mention merely because they wear a curious costume, consisting of a short coat, of a dark green, with a red collar, and deep gold lace, and a round cap on the head, with a

gold plate in front, and a bundle of black ostrich
feathers falling on one side, with which they never
part company.' It is, in fact, this round cap with a
gold plate in front, and a bunch of black ostrich
plumes falling on one side, which is characteristic of
the skorokhods. At that date it would sound as
though there were some scores of them in the Imperial household, since they were in attendance,
also, upon the Dowager Empress; and, even in
1828, they were looked upon as persons from a fairy
story.

Of this most complete and glorious of Courts
so little trace is left. There are no published works:
no albums of lithographed drawings, although its
existence, on a scale more elaborate than that of
Louis XIV, is so recent. Thus it comes about that
the skorokhods are vanished completely. Only in
that huge folio of Alexander II's coronation is their
image preserved, in the banquet scene. Two or
three of them stand against the walls, in idleness,
but nearly hidden by the crowd so that the detail of
their costume is all but obscured. In a far corner of
the room another bunch of black feathers nods upon
one side, but no more of the skorokhod can be seen.
He is hidden by a Court Arab and a group of

foreign diplomats. The Court Arabs, likewise, are gone without a trace. This folio volume is the only document that shows the colours of their costume. With the skorokhods there is something equivocal in their appearance. If we now transfer ourselves from the library to the fictitious reality that is before our eyes, having but studied the book for reference and in order to be correct in detail, we come back to the supper rooms and behold the skorokhods standing by the empty chairs. Their high cheek bones and clean shaven faces, in this time of beards and whiskers, make them like male dancers. It is, perhaps, fanciful to think there is something of that in their movements; but, certainly, they walk with a soft tread, while their feathered caps have the touch of Hermes from an old masque. Hermes was messenger of the gods and of Jupiter in particular. The skorokhods are Court runners of the Tsar. Such is the analogy; and in dress and feature they conform to it.

After supper, dancing begins again. The Grand Duchesses now have their moment, like the swan princesses, and each sends her Court Cavalier to inform the partner whom she has chosen. There is time to walk through the different rooms. Not that they are beautiful in themselves, but in the blazing candle light they make a splendid setting; and if some rooms are empty while the ball goes on, it is possible for the moment to admire nothing else than the vases and candelabra of precious marbles. In one room, a pair of stands for candelabra of violet jasper from Siberia: tables of porphyry and malachite: further on, more violet jasper in the form of vases or great tazze: vases and tables of lapis lazuli: more stands for candelabra of rose-coloured porphyry, or rhodonite: tazze of syenite and aventurine: a vase of Siberian jasper of a lilac colour: a jasper tazza and a pair of candelabra, seven feet high, recently arrived from Ekaterinburg: a tazza of hard marble, from Siberia, of a green tint with flesh-coloured streakings: and another of pale flesh-coloured aventurine. All of modern workmanship, not earlier than the reign of Nicholas I, and mostly from the Ural mountains. The marbles of the ancient world would seem, in imagery, to owe their beauty to volcanic fire, or to the sun of Africa or Asia. These, of Siberia and the Urals, are of an ice age. Their action has been glacial and not volcanic: both in the marbles and in the minerals. Of the crystals and semi-precious stones, worn as jewels,

CRYSTALS AND SEMI-PRECIOUS STONES
much might be written. Beryls and aquamarines:
blue crystals of Murzinsk in Siberia: flesh-coloured
crystals: beryls of an emerald colour: brown or
yellow topaz: tourmalines, and the rose-coloured
sort, called rubellite: uvarovites, or emerald green
garnets: chrysoberyls from Siberia, called Alex-
andrites, emerald green by daylight, but lilac or
amethystine if held before a candle: Siberian ame-
thysts, and many others. The interior of the Winter
Palace is remarkable more for its tables and vases of
rare marbles than for its works of art. And the halls
of the Hermitage, for all their wonders, are no less
rich in this. They all come from the Imperial mines
and quarries, and are worked in the Imperial work-
shops. They are, in some sort, the wonders of Asia,
but of the cold half of that continent, and in harmony with the fur-trimmed robes and high lambskin hats of Tartar, Circassian, or Bokharan noble.

It is getting late. Come back, for the last time, into
the ballroom! The wax lights are half-burned down,
which throws a nearer glitter upon the dancers and
draws the fire out of the diamonds. More especially
in the mazurka. Because the dancers halt to the
music, and go down upon one knee. There is a
great concourse watching, and footmen walk among

them with trays of drinks and ices: 'l'officiers de bouche portent l'habit rouge; la livrée est verte, avec l'aigle noir à deux têtes brodès sur un galon d'or.' In the next rooms, within sound of the music, there are Aladdin's chambers, treasuries of sweets and cakes made in the pastry kitchens of the Winter Palace in a variety and profusion that could fill a chapter to themselves. Many are inventions of the eighteenth century, sorbets and chocolates of French origin, but these have been surpassed in the extrava-gance of the Russian genius. Every morning a stand is brought up to the rooms of each Court lady living in the palace, whether here or in the country palaces, and this has eight or ten trays of sweets upon the tiers. Nearly all of them will go down at night uneaten. It is the prerogative of the servants to sell these cakes and sweets, and the best confectioners of the capital are supplied by them. In this manner it is possible for private persons to be served from the Imperial kitchens. On an evening such as this the Court pastrycooks have surpassed themselves. There are, as well, fruits and jellies, and grey-grained caviar of the finest sort. Huge blocks of ice, the size of a small iceberg, have been hollowed out to hold tubs with bottles of champagne. And flowers and

palms ornament these sideboards and reach half‑
way to the ceiling, so that it is like a childhood's
dream. Bishops and archimandrites are among
those who help themselves, standing in a group at a
table near a door into the ballroom. An archbishop,
or one of the highest dignitaries of the Church, is at
this moment talking to the Dowager‑Empress in
the ballroom, with his ecclesiastics in a group be‑
hind him. All the bishops wear the high white veil,
the white kloboúk, falling from the crown of their
hats upon their shoulders and concealing their long
hair. They wear violet or black robes. All have
beards of great length and wear their hair long like
women, some, in fact, would have curling masses
of snow‑white hair down to their waists. But, in the
crowd of military uniforms and ladies wearing
Court dress and the kokoshnik, what is peculiar in
these priests is their snow‑white veils; till we re‑
member the frozen Neva and the snow outside, and
they become snow martens, Arctic foxes. Their
white beards and white veils are in symbol of this
land of winter. It is apparent, also, that they have
been chosen for their height, or are a race apart. And
we think of them driving back in sledges, three
horses abreast, to their monasteries.

Priests or monks, and the military, are part of all
ritual under the Tsars. In ceremonial, whether it be
the coronation, a banquet, or a ball, the Tsar's bodyguard have particular emphasis put upon them. It
is only now, in the light of this, that certain figures
find their explanation. They are of two kinds; and
have been seen in the crowd and on the dancing
floor. In their stiff magnificence they could be
knights of a military order, for this is, indeed, probably the most splendid uniform ever invented. It
is the full dress uniform of the Chevalier Gardes and
the Gardes à cheval. Their white tunics and silver
or gilt breastplates, respectively, are already familiar.
It is in this garb that they mount the picket before
the Malachite Room. But the officers on duty at the
ball are subtly differenced. Instead of the cuirass
they wear the super-vest. This is a scarlet waistcoat
worn over their white tunics; and for the Chevalier
Gardes, in front and on the back, it has the star of
the Order of St. Andrew. The super-vest is sleeve-
less, so that the white sleeves of the tunic can be
seen; and it has a scalloped edge at the waist which
is lined with blue, the colour of the ribbon of the
Order, while the collar is blue, also, and a thin line
or piping of blue, on each side, runs from the

shoulder to the waist. In the case of the Gardes à
cheval the super-vest is scarlet with large golden
eagles on the front and back. The officers of both
regiments posted to this interior duty, on guard, or
as dancing partners at the ball, wear black Wellington boots and white elk skin breeches. They carry
their eagle crested helms. The officer who is on
sentinel duty in the Winter Palace remains there for
twenty-four hours. He is allowed an armchair; and
may undo the chain of his helmet and take off one
glove. Less could not be expected of Sir Galahad!
The elk skin breeches were exceedingly uncom-
fortable, worn next to the skin, and could not be
put on or taken off without two soldiers to assist. It
was necessary that they should be damped and
smeared with soap in order that there should be no
crease in them. Certainly the super-vest had its
difficulties, also. In the aggregate, the effect is magnificent, but most curious in ingredient. The elk skin
breeches are those of the Northern hunter, but
carried to the parade level, and dating in their meaning from the wars of Charles XII and the Tsar
Peter. Definitely, in fact, of Northern origin, of the
elk forest, not tiger or lion skin of the tropics. In
place of the cuirass, for indoor duty, they wear the

super-vest, which is a parallel to the surcoat of the Middle Ages, but suggests that the Knight or Paladin is under extreme scrutiny through the day and night. All the eyes of the tournament are upon him, whether it be a banquet or a ball. And it has been given an almost religious significance by the star of St. Andrew, as though he is Knight of a military order, even a Crusader, if a Chevalier Garde; and, if a Garde à cheval, that the double-headed eagles of Byzantium upon his super-vest are the heraldic device of his sovereign, for all that may intend. Their eagle crested helmets, whether gold or silver, in this setting have nothing classical about them. They are knight's helms; and by reason of some vow all the knights have dressed the same. The date of this uniform, with the super-vest, is the reign of Nicholas I, and surely it takes rank with the literary or aesthetic achievements of that time. The officers dance, holding their helmets on one arm; but it does not interfere even in the mazurka, to which, indeed the stamping of their boots and jingling of their spurs give the necessary and martial emphasis. In the Polish mazurka the cavaliers should twirl their long moustaches. But that is in the national character. The Poles shaved their heads and wore long moustaches. They twirled these: or put a hand upon the pommel of their swords. The Chevalier Gardes, or their rivals, are more stiff and formal. There are no long flowing garments, or fur trimmed robes. The super-vest is instead of a breastplate; and they hold a heavy helmet on their arm. The Russian mazurka in the Winter Palace is, in fact, military, more than martial. But the stranger might wonder who are the paladins upon the dancing floor. The gesture of dancing with a helmet on the arm is as though the dance is a ritual, as much as war or prayer. And the long galleries echo to the mazurka.

But the music stops. There is an interval, a silence, before the metamorphosis. A change is coming. Though the wax lights glitter, this is the darkness before the transformation. Outside, the snow is falling. That is certain. Here, the camellia and orange trees are in blossom, and will be taken back, tomorrow, to the hothouses. The mazurka and the polonaise are spent. We have not heard the waltz.

It will come. When the ballroom is empty, per-haps, and the dancers have driven home in their sledges! When the air will be laden only with the other flowers and the camellia, which is scentless. How much will have fled then! It will be too late. The waltz is not yet written. But it was born of such a night as this, breathing from the flowers, and transforming living persons. It begins. We hear it coming. The opening or preluding is slow and gentle. It offers its different phases in this beginning, one after another, which will transform themselves and lead the dance. Slowly, slowly, and coming to a standstill, and a sweeping and soaring of the harp-strings, up and up, hovering at the flower mouth. In this throbbing of the harpstrings the waltz intoxi-cates itself: it tries its plumes, and comes down, not to a standstill, but into position, ready for the dance.

The opening phrase of the waltz, known and loved since childhood, with that accent on the second line or couplet of the repetition, which gives the rhythm; and after much flourishing, its return again, no longer pleading but confident, mounting and mounting, no longer androgynous but mascu-line, and carrying all before it with its fire. Who does not love the Valse des Fleurs and cannot listen to it with our loving ears! But it starts again, in fuller and more plangent statement, with more de-tailed phrasing, and a fuller orchestration. This is

148

the feminine exposition, the hen bird, wren or nightingale, the woman in the rose. And it is the moment to come away into the empty rooms; and look out through the window on to the frozen Neva. Every window in the Winter Palace glitters with lights, and the ice floes answer back. The preening and soaring of the Valse des Fleurs reaches us from the ballroom. How lovely and familiar its plumes and scented petals! We listen in an intoxication. The phrases are so clear and beautiful and the waltz is in full movement, round and round; nothing ordinary, inspired and exotic, miraculous in little, like the camellia petals, which can be white or red, or striped like the women's dresses. What a hot-house Tchaikowsky inhabited in his inspiration: of stephanotis, gloxinia, lapageria! This waltz can be scented like a gardenia, plucked from its tree, still damp with the water on it. Or more tropical plants: crotons or nepenthes, only for their sound, not for their scent, and for the heat they dwell in. It is the Valse des Fleurs: but they have bright and varie-gated leaves.

Forget the music for a moment and look out on the night! There are thousands of persons, men and women, in Siberian prisons. Four years ago, in 1864 the Polish rebellion was bloodily suppressed. Here are the names of martyrs: Sierakowski, mortally wounded in action, and hanged by Muraviev when on the point of death: Cieszkowski, wounded in battle, and killed in bed next day: Padlewski and Frankowski, wounded, taken prisoners, and executed with their bandaged heads: the butcher Muraviev killed thousands more, and exiled to Siberia in their tens of thousands. There are many in prison: and many starving, of Russian flesh and blood. How much longer will it continue! For forty years and more. Until the end: or the awakening. Wickedness or ignorance? There is no answer.

And the intoxication of the waltz returns, manoeuvring for the climax. More pellucid and crystalline than ever in its orchestration; lovely in every little detail. It dances in itself, and shakes its lilies. The coda quickens even the dead walls into the waltz, turning, turning, in an ecstasy, a delirium. For it is the Valse des Fleurs which with a last crescendo leaves the dancers on their feet. It is the end of the ball. The procession has gone back again into its apartments. The Court Arabs close the doors of the Malachite Room behind them. The skorokhods, like dancers disguised as birds, usher the guests towards the different stairs. And, only now, their masters having retired, the Minister of the Court, the Masters of Ceremonies, and the Marshal of the Court, wand in hand, go up to the next floor, where their supper is ready for them. It is an exit up a Bibiena staircase when the Sleeping Beauty has been put to sleep. And they talk far into another snowflake dawn. Lights in the other windows are put out, one by one. The camellia sleeps. But all in their dreams, tonight, will hear the waltz. It is music that will never die.